# DANGEROUS JOBS

# DANGEROUS JOBS

## THE WORLD'S RISKIEST WAYS TO MAKE AN EXTRA BUCK

### ABIGAIL R. GEHRING

Skyhorse Publishing

Skyhorse Publishing books may be purchased in bulk at special discounts for sales promotion, corporate gifts, fund-raising, or educational purposes. Special editions can also be created to specifications. For details, contact the Special Sales Department, Skyhorse Publishing, 555 Eighth Avenue, Suite 903, New York, NY 10018 or info@skyhorsepublishing.com.

www.skyhorsepublishing.com

10 9 8 7 6 5 4 3 2 1

Library of Congress Cataloging-in-Publication Data

Gehring, Abigail R.
Dangerous jobs / Abigail Gehring.
p. cm.
ISBN 978-1-60239-620-3
1. Hazardous occupations. I. Title.
HD7262.G49 2009
331.702--dc22

2009002028

Printed in China

"You gain strength, courage, and confidence by every experience in which you really stop to look fear in the face. You must do the thing which you think you cannot do."

—Eleanor Roosevelt

# Contents

# Introduction

There is something undeniably alluring about danger. It's the rush of power that comes with a surge of mind-numbing, muscle-twitching adrenaline. The addictive sense of relief that washes over you after you've survived a terrifying ordeal. It's the stuff of legends, of tall tales, of the stories you still love to tell about yourself from childhood. Amusement parks bank on people enjoying fear enough to spend a hefty wad of cash and hours standing in line just to experience it for a few heart-pounding moments. Hollywood rakes in the cash with every blockbuster thriller it produces, even if the acting is terrible and the plot more predictable than Chuck Norris winning a fight.

But the fact that you're reading this book means that you probably appreciate the glories of danger even more than most. You're not satisfied with the occasional roller coaster ride or with watching reruns of *Fear Factor* late at night. You want more. You want to pursue danger like it's your job.

Well, now's your chance. What have you got to lose (besides maybe an arm, the ability to reproduce, or . . .)? The everyday normal job market is lousy, everyone's flippng out about the economy, and if you're one of the 55 percent of Americans who consider themselves "unengaged" in their current place of employment,[1] you're freaking bored. So try something different, like lion taming, for example. I haven't met a single lion trainer who's been laid off in the past months of economic turmoil. Architects, yes. Bankers, yes. But lion tamers? Not a single one. Now that's job security! (Which is ironic if you think about it because security is sort of the opposite of danger . . .) But really, even if lion taming isn't your cup of tea, there are a lot fewer people scrambling for jobs that are decidedly dangerous, so if you have a flair for the frightening, you should jump at the opportunity to turn your passion into profit.

Plus, a lot of dangerous jobs pay well. (Not all of them, unfortunately. Cashiers have one of the most dangerous jobs in America, and they generally get minimum wage—see page 31. That sucks.) The military is currently offering sign-on bonuses of up to $40,000. Not too shabby. And if you're into flying planes that might have mechanical problems, consider becoming an experimental test pilot for a solid six-figure salary (page 72).

And now it's time for my disclaimer. Although I'm as big a fan of adventure as the next chick, I'm not actually encouraging you to become a mercenary or to join the bomb squad. I mean, if you want to do it, more power to you. But please don't come whining to me when you get your leg blown off (though feel free to send me some cash if you get rich—you can reach me through the publisher). This book is meant to

---

[1] This statistic is from workopolis.com. Check it out. Especially if you're bored at work right now and you're dying for something interesting to read . . . besides this book, of course.

present the facts, offer some inspiration, and give you the kick in the butt you need to find yourself a cool job. Oh, and while we're talking about facts . . . I've tried to offer clear, concise, and accurate information for every job entry in this book, but since I'm not a prophet (which can be a very dangerous job, by the way—Jonah got swallowed by a whale), by the time this book is in your hands some of my current facts may have become historical facts. Sorry about that.

So have fun, try to stay alive, and good luck on your new adventures!

# DANGEROUS JOBS

## THE WORLD'S RISKIEST WAYS TO MAKE AN EXTRA BUCK

Armored Car Guard

# Armored Car Guard

### What You Do
Drive a bullet-resistant armored car full of cash or valuable materials. Often you'll be making deliveries to or picking up cash from banks or ATMs.

### Why It's Risky
When someone sees an armored car, it's pretty obvious there's something of value inside. This makes you a prime target for attack as you are the main thing standing between the robber and the goods. You'll be especially vulnerable when you step out of the vehicle, either to pick up or deliver the valuables or to take a break from driving.

### What You Need
You'll need to pass a firearm training course, have a clean record and a driver's license, and probably a recommendation or three to ensure your integrity.

**The Payoff**

$10 to $20/hour. And—if you're (un)lucky enough to get robbed and live—some great stories.

**Sites to Check Out**

- **www.dunbararmored.com**—An armored-car company that operates in cities around the world. They might want to hire you. You won't know unless you ask!

- **www.toolboxtopics.com/Programs/Safety Programs/Armored Car Services.doc**—An Internet document from Florida Department of Labor's Division of Safety, detailing safety procedures for driving, first aid, and the use of firearms.

- **www.self-defender.net/extras/transport-security.htm**—Transport security tips for armored-car drivers in the case of an on-the-job emergency.

## Bicycle Messenger

**What You Do**

You'll carry and deliver packages and letters around an urban area, via bicycle. Hand deliveries by bike are faster than walking or driving in a gridlocked city, which means you'll always be in demand. Messengers are particularly popular in Beijing and Buenos Aires.

**Why It's Risky**

Motorists generally dislike cyclists, which is bad because they're the ones with air bags. Case in point: a D.C. attorney representing a bike messenger who had been hit by a car had to interview potential jury members for *days* because no one could claim they were completely impartial. They'd all already sided with the driver who injured the messenger.

Weather also poses a threat to your health, as exposure to rain, snow, or wind increases

Bicycle Messenger

your susceptibility to colds or the flu. Bad road conditions also pose a risk, especially if the vehicles around you are losing control due to wet or icy pavement.

### What You Need

You'll need a bicycle and bag to carry packages in; both should cost you under $200. A bag with a single strap that goes diagonally across your chest is convenient as it slides from front to back without you having to remove it. You'll also need a helmet. Radio systems, if used, are generally provided by the service you work for. You'll definitely need to be fit to make it past your first few days. If you plan on having a regular work schedule, remember that you'll be riding a bicycle for forty hours every week. Think of all the gym membership money you'll save!

### The Payoff

The demand for bicycle messengers has gone down over the last few decades, as fax machines and e-mail have created speedier communication. However, pay has gone up, and you can expect a commission of $5 to $15 a delivery. If you have steady work you'll make about $300/week.

**Sites to Check Out**

- **www.messengers.org**—The International Federation of Bike Messengers, with links to messenger companies and associations worldwide.

- **www.messmedia.org**—The Messenger Institute for Media Accuracy offers interesting articles, useful tips such as how to choose a good messenger bag, and a downloadable version of the Messenger Industry Handbook.

- **www.cmwc2008.com/index.html**—The Cycle Messenger World Championships (CMWC) Web site for the 2008 games held in Toronto. Learn about events like the Cargo Race and Bike Polo, see the results, and check out their great messenger links. Start planning now for the 2009 Championships in Tokyo!

## Bodyguard

### What You Do

Basically, you'll be a babysitter for grown-ups (without the diaper changing). Usually the grown-up will be a VIP, such as a famous actor or actress or a high-profile political figure, but your responsibilities will be basically the same as when you were sixteen and watching your neighbor's toddler. Only now, instead of carrying a diaper bag, you'll be toting a gun. Your job is to keep your charge out of harm's way, and maybe drive him or her around the neighborhood for play dates (a.k.a. business meetings) and such.

### Why It's Risky

The danger comes because VIPs don't like to be treated as toddlers. So rather than holding the celebrity's hand as she crosses the street, you'll probably have to walk a few paces behind, which in turn may mean throwing yourself in

Bodyguard

front of a moving car at the last second because she's yakking on her cell and doesn't notice she's in the middle of the road. If it's a bullet rather than a car headed toward your charge, you'll still have to get between the two. And you'll always need to keep an eye out for sticky fingers, because playground bullies grow up, and PDAs with valuable information or mink coats with wads of cash in the pockets, are even more alluring than sandbox toys.

### What You Need

VIPs are, by definition, very important persons, so it's understandable that they'd demand more of their bodyguards than most parents do of their babysitters. For example, it's helpful if you have a background in the armed forces, security, prison guard services, and/or martial arts. You'll need a driver's license, probably, and if you're a criminal don't bother applying—you're probably making more money doing whatever you're doing now anyway.

### The Payoff

If you're guarding someone very important, it's probably because you're very qualified, and you can expect to make a six-figure salary. But your average bodyguard will be more likely to make $40,000–$70,000/year.

**Sites to Check Out**

- **www.bodyguardcareers.com**—Find job listings, info on bodyguard schools, and bodyguard-related stories here.

- **www.bodyguardblog.com**—Get the inside scoop on life as a bodyguard.

- **www.bodyguard-training.org**—Tips for being a successful bodyguard.

**Inspiration**

"Don't waste life in doubts and fears; spend yourself on the work before you, well assured that right performance of this hour's duties will be the best preparation for the hours and ages that will follow it."

**—Ralph Waldo Emerson**

# Bomb Squad

### What You Do

Find and destroy bombs. If there's a bomb threat at a school, airport, or anywhere, you'll have to go into the building as everyone else is being hurried out. If you're an explosives expert in the army, your job is even more dangerous, as there's a good chance your call to action is due to more than a pimply teenager with self-esteem issues scrawling "I'm going to blow you all up!" on a napkin. (Not that such a threat shouldn't be taken seriously . . . one never knows these days.) Check out *Bomb Squad: A Year Inside the Nation's Most Exclusive Police Unit* (you can find it on Google Books) for more details.

### Why It's Risky

Duh, these are *bombs* we're talking about.

Bomb Squad

**What You Need**
To work in the bomb squad as part of the police force, you have to have a squeaky-clean record (no drugs, no proof you helped your underage nephew get beer, definitely no felonies); pass a lie-detector test; be in good physical shape, including good vision; and be willing to be on twenty-four-hour call, even on major holidays. To be a bomb disposal expert in the army, you'll have to go through thirty-eight weeks of Advanced Individual Training (in addition to nine weeks of Basic Training).

**The Payoff**
Anywhere from $40,000–$100,000/year, depending on experience and location.

**Sites to Check Out**
• **www.wired.com/wired/archive/13.11/bomb. html**—An interesting article about a day in the life of the "Baghdad Bomb Squad."

• **www.pbs.org/wgbh/nova/robots**—Get a handle on your competition—bomb-disposing robots.

• **www.xm-materials.com/k9_bomb_dog. html**—The New York City bomb squad training manual.

## Border Patrol Agent

### What You Do

You'll be responsible for preventing illegal aliens and contraband from crossing the borders into the United States. Border patrol is increasingly focusing their attention on detecting and stopping terrorists from entering the country, as well as preventing child trafficking, and, of course, keeping out illegal drugs. You might be riding horseback in southern Texas, monitoring luggage with security personnel in Miami International Airport, or checking passports in northern Vermont. Border patrol operates around the perimeter of the United States and within its borders in certain high-risk areas.

### Why It's Risky

There's a good chance you'll be working along sparsely populated borders, oftentimes alone. One agent was patrolling in the Otay Mountains when he spotted a group of illegal immigrants

Border Patrol Agent

attempting to cross into San Diego. They scattered when they realized that he was an agent, he chased them, and moments later he slipped (or was pushed) off the mountainside and fell 150 feet to his death.

Harsh climates in the hot deserts near Mexico and along desolate stretches of the Canadian border pose health risks, compounded by irregular and often long hours. And it's not uncommon for agents to be pelted by rocks or even gunned down by immigrants determined not to be stopped.

### What You Need
You must be a U.S. citizen, under forty years of age, fluent in Spanish or able to learn it (you will be given the Artificial Language Test to determine your language-learning ability), possess a valid driver's license, and pass a thorough background investigation, medical examination, fitness test, and drug test. You may also be subject to a polygraph examination.

### The Payoff
$36,000 to $47,000 is the standard entry-level salary. You will also receive a uniform allowance of $1,500, excellent overtime pay, life insurance, health insurance, retirement benefits, and a savings plan.

**Sites to Check Out**
- **www.cbp.gov**—The U.S. Customs and Border Protection official site (check out the FAQs page).

- **www.borderpatrol.gov**—Find job listings, recruiting events, and more information here.

- **http://newsfromtheborder.blogspot.com**— This blog is not for the weak of heart. Although the blog has a religious angle, most of the posts focus on run-ins with gunmen, smugglers, kidnappers, and bandits, many of which are disturbing (to say the least).

## Lingo

*CBP*—Customs and Border Protection, a.k.a. border patrol.

*Coyotes*—Guides who help illegal immigrants over the border. It's a lucrative job, but even more dangerous than being a border patrol agent.

*SBI*—Secure Borders Initiative, a program launched in 1995 focuses on integrating border security programs and using technology, personnel, and infrastructure to prevent terrorist attacks and other transnational crimes.

# Bounty Hunter

### What You Do

When a criminal jumps bail and disappears, it's your job to track him or her down. First you'll research the fugitive, talk to his or her friends or family, follow their leads, and probably spend a lot of time patrolling the area(s) where you think the fugitive is residing. Then, when the moment is right, you'll arrest the runaway and bring him or her to the closest jail, or, in some states, call the cops and have them perform the arrest.

### Why It's Risky

You'll likely be spending a lot of your time in bad neighborhoods. If the criminal himself doesn't beat you up or shoot you to avoid arrest, you might get mugged or molested by another thug. It's likely that the fugitive's pals are not teddy-bear types, either, and they're the ones you'll need to be chatting with to get the clues for your treasure hunt.

### What You Need

Rules for bounty hunters vary from state to state. At the least, you'll need a copy of the "bail piece," the paperwork stating that the person you're chasing is indeed a fugitive. For most states you won't need a warrant for arrest, nor will you need to read the fugitive his or her rights. You may need to be licensed, or you might just need to get yourself registered. You'll probably want to carry a gun on the job (assuming you're licensed to do so), but think before you use it. You'll only get the reward money if you bring the captive back alive.

Bounty Hunter

**The Payoff**

10 to 20 percent of the fugitive's bail.

**Sites to Check Out**

- **http://beabountyhunter.com**—You probably don't need to take a course to become a bounty hunter, but this educational site has a lot of useful information and articles besides the seminar and course offerings.

- **www.bountyhunteremployment.com**—Check out the FAQ page on this site for basic information on becoming a bounty hunter.

- **www.dogthebountyhunter.com**—Official site of the most famous present-day bounty hunter, Dog.

**Inspiration**

"We triumph without glory when we conquer without danger."

**—Corneille**

# Building Construction Worker

**What You Do**

Whether you're working on a home renovation project or a skyscraper, you'll be putting your shop skills to the test, sawing, hammering, lugging materials, and possibly operating heavy-duty machinery (which you probably didn't get to do in shop class). You might work for a construction company or as an independent contractor.

**Why It's Risky**

Considering you'll probably be working around cranes and forklifts, possibly dealing with wiring and electricity, climbing tall ladders and scaling steep roofs (even in bad weather), balancing on scaffolding, and lifting heavy boards, bags of cement, or bricks, it would be kind of amazing if you didn't get hurt one way or another. It's really no wonder construction has the third highest rate of death by injury, according

Building Construction Worker

to the National Institute for Occupational Safety and Health.

## What You Need

You must be able-bodied and willing to participate in real physical labor. For many positions, no formal education is required, although specialists (carpenters, bricklayers, plumbers, etc.) are often trained by attending a technical or trade school or by doing an apprenticeship.

## The Payoff

Expect to earn between $13 and $20/hour, more if you're experienced in a specialized trade, such as plumbing. You'll probably score some serious back and arm muscles, too.

## Sites to Check Out

- **www.homebuildingmanual.com/Glossary. htm**—Do you know what astragal is? How about Romex? This glossary will tell you.

- **www.constructionjobs.com**—Start your job search here (though if you live in a rural area, looking for job listings in the local newspaper may be more effective).

- **http://constructionadvice.org**—Free construction information and advice, mostly regarding home construction and remodeling.

Butcher

### What You Do

You'll use knives, power saws, and other equipment to cut, trim, grind, and chop meat. You may be responsible for ordering meats, unloading carcasses from delivery trucks, mantaining machinery, and possibly overseeing other butchers.

### Why It's Risky

Floors in meat-cutting rooms are frequently slippery with blood and fat. When you're carrying heavy carcasses and you're surrounded with sharp things, this poses a serious risk. In addition, these rooms are kept cold to preserve the meat, and cold hands are not always very nimble when operating band saws and sl

### What You Need

Butchers are generally trained on the job, so formal education or previous experience is not necessary for most entry-level positions.

Butcher

You will need to be strong enough to carry heavy loads and operate large machinery. This job is not recommended for vegetarians, or any sort of animal-lover, for that matter.

### The Payoff
Around $30,000/year. If you're working for a supermarket you'll probably also get health benefits and paid vacations.

### Sites to Check Out
- **www.meatami.org**—The American Meat Institute.

- **www.ufcw.org**—United Food and Commercial Workers International Union, CLC.

- **http://animalscience.unl.edu/meats/id/**— The University of Nebraska offers a very helpful list of all the various cuts of meat and pictures of what they look like.

### Inspiration

"Every time we choose safety, we reinforce fear."

**—Cheri Huber**

## Cabdriver

### What You Do

Cabdrivers work primarily in urban areas because, of course, that's where there are lots of people who need rides. You'll cruise around, waiting to be flagged down by a weary pedestrian, figure out where they want to go (sometimes easier said than done, especially if *they're* not exactly sure where they want to go), and take them there.

### Why It's Risky

You work alone, probably often at odd hours of the night, and if you're even mildly successful, you have a stash of cash riding with you. If there's someone else wanting that cash badly enough, there's not much stopping them from hitting you over the head and taking it. Not to mention the general dangers of driving in congested areas (i.e., crashing).

**What You Need**

If you're in England, you'll need to study for two to four years and take a bunch of tests before you can become a legal cabdriver. Becoming a cabbie in the United States doesn't require quite so much patience. Training is likely to take a few days rather than a few years. You will need a valid driver's license and a relatively clean driving record, and probably pass a drug test. Some cities also require a chauffeur license.

The easiest way to get a taxicab is to lease it from a taxi company in your area. They usually

Cabdriver

rent out cars for a twelve-hour period and you won't have to worry about getting your own insurance, oil changes, or other general maintenance.

### The Payoff

How much you earn will depend on a lot of factors, including how personable you are (much of your income will come from tips) and what area you're driving in. But the average in the United States is $30,000–$40,000/year.

### Sites to Check Out

- **www.taxi-library.org/gord28.htm**—Useful tips for staying alive.

- **www.nycabbie.com/stories.html**—Stories from taxi drivers all over the world and those who have benefited from their services. Also has a help column that is seemingly unrelated to the world of cab driving except for the name, "Dear Cabbie."

- **http://cabsareforkissing.blogspot.com**— Entertaining blog about life as a taxi driver in New York City.

## Cashier

### What You Do

You'll take people's money in exchange for whatever it is the store or restaurant sells. It's pretty simple, but you'll have to stand for long periods of time and sometimes deal with obnoxious customers. You might get perks like an employee discount or free sodas.

### Why It's Risky

You'll work by yourself, or maybe in a small group, and be in charge of a lot of money. Unfortunately, this makes you and your coworkers targets for greedy nutjobs. Three hundred and thirty-six retail trade fatalities occurred in 2007 from occupational injury or homicide, with forty deaths at convenience stores, forty-two at gas stations, and fifteen at clothing and jewelry stores. According to the National Institute for Occupational Safety and Health, "The second highest number of workplace fatalities among workers younger than age 18 occurred in the

Cashier

retail trades (e.g., restaurants and retail stores). Between 1992 and 2000, 63 percent of these deaths were due to assaults and violent acts, most of which were homicides."

### What You Need

You have to be at least fourteen years old and have a work permit. If you are under sixteen, federal law prevents you from working more than eighteen hours in a school week and forty hours in a nonschool week. And, with all seriousness, gel inserts for your shoes.

### The Payoff

Most cashiers make minimum wage, which is $6.55. However, some states require employers to pay more or less than the federal rate, and cashiers at high-end stores may make considerably more.

### Sites to Check Out

• **money.cnn.com/magazines/fortune/bestcompanies/2008**—The 2008 *Fortune* magazine list of "100 Best Companies to Work For" included Starbucks, The Container Store, Nordstrom, Whole Foods, Wegmans, and Publix supermarkets.

• **www.jobster.com**—An easy-to-use job posting site that can search any state in the United States.

- **http://www.snagajob.com/job-buddies/ cashier.aspx**—A teen-focused guide on getting a job as a cashier. Bonus: you can also search openings in your area on Snagajob.

**Chef**

### What You Do

You'll plan a menu and prepare food for diners in your restaurant or café. If you are the executive chef, you will oversee your team (line cooks, sous chef, pastry chef, etc.) and make sure everything runs smoothly in the kitchen.

### Why It's Risky

Restaurant kitchens are generally high-stress, fast-paced environments with an overabundance of sharp knives and flames. The combination can be deadly. Or if not deadly, it could at least cost you a finger. During a recent four-year survey, 6,700 restaurant employees had a fingertip or digit amputated. Many other cooks suffered burns or falls from slippery floors, and one aspiring chef had a heart attack after eating too much of his own spicy chili. Keep in mind when considering a restaurant for employment that, generally, the less expensive the fare, the

Chef

more lax the kitchen staff, and the more risk of losing a finger, or worse.

### What You Need

You should start getting experience in the food industry as soon as possible, even if you're not handling food, to get an idea of how a restaurant works. Make food at home to practice and perfect the basic techniques and recipes. Your own kitchen is the best place to experiment (if it doesn't come out right you won't have any angry customers!). The standard career path is culinary school, followed by working your way up the ladder, and finally applying for certification by the American Culinary Federation. The ACF requires you to choose a level of certification, submit an application with proof of your training and experience, take a written exam, and then perform a practical exam at an approved test site.

### The Payoff

Figures from the National Restaurant Association show that executive chefs have a median salary of $50,000, and the median for sous and pastry chefs is approximately $31,000. The Bureau of Labor Statistics sets the average hourly wage for chefs and head cooks as $19.57, or about $40,000 a year. If you work in an urban area, or for a particularly well-known establishment, you'll definitely make more than the median. In addition, your ACF certificate will help increase your salary.

**Sites to Check Out**

- **www.restaurant.org**—The National Restaurant Association Web site has just about everything relating to the restaurant industry, from politics that affect businesses and food safety training to an online "Job Bank" and community outreach programs.

- **www.acfchefs.org**—The American Culinary Federation was founded in 1929 and has more than 22,000 members nationwide. They helped change the culinary industry by elevating "chef" to a professional level when the title was added to the Department of Labor's Dictionary of Official Titles in 1976.

- **www.foodnetwork.com**—The Food Network site is a great companion to their programming, with a library of recipes from their shows that you can try out. Television isn't exactly a replacement for culinary school, but at the very least it's inspirational.

## CIA Agent

**What You Do**

If I told you, I'd have to kill you. But you seem like a nice person (you did buy this book) so I'll fill you in. The majority of Agency employees have desk jobs, but when most people think "CIA agent" they have in mind the Clandestine Service. You will "collect information that is not obtainable through other means" that is pertinent to American foreign policy and national security. You might be performing counterintelligence if the president authorizes it.

However, if you don't want to be James (or Jane) Bond, you still have options. The Directorate of Intelligence (DI) collects and analyzes information, which means you could be translating a document, projecting a country's economy and weapons development in the next decade, evaluating satellite photos, even briefing the president on recent developments. Remember Q from those Bond movies? The Directorate of

CIA Agent

Science and Technology (DS&T) is the place for aspiring techies. You'll analyze data, research or design advanced technologies, train agents to use these inventions, and even work in the field alongside the Clandestine Service. They need lawyers, media relations staff—there's even an Entertainment Industry Liaison!

### Why It's Risky
The CIA looks for the most patriotic, loyal, and trustworthy people in the nation, then entrusts them with top-secret information. The risky part is not only getting that information, but also knowing it. Being a spy is extremely dangerous, but being a captured spy with valuable knowledge? Not a happy situation.

### What You Need
The hiring procedure for any CIA job is very rigorous, and even the most qualified people can be turned down for a number of reasons. Don't tell anyone you're applying because it will undermine your cover before you even start. You must have U.S. citizenship and a squeaky-clean record. You should be drug free, as the Agency requires no illegal drug use twelve months prior to your application, and any use before that will be seriously evaluated. Any criminal activity on your record will seriously undermine your résumé.

If you don't have a college degree, start working on it. A bachelor's degree is required for almost all jobs, and some might request advanced degrees. Take serious classes and get good grades. If you are not bilingual, take foreign language classes. Learn a language that's spoken in a political "hot spot" such as Farsi, Arabic, Chinese, or Russian. The CIA looks favorably on military experience, as you may already have security clearance plus certain physical and mental capabilities. They'll do an extraordinarily thorough background check, which can take over a year (they'll make sure you didn't lie in your application, don't cheat on your spouse, have good credit, no questionable alliances or past—*everything*). You'll have to pass medical and psychological exams, a polygraph test, and if you get a conditional offer, pass your initial training. Yes, they're thorough.

### The Payoff

Your salary will depend on your position and experience. For example, an analyst job will likely pay $46,000 to $90,000—that means you could make up to $44,000 more a year if you're more experienced. Even in the most dangerous CIA positions, don't expect to make a six-figure salary. You can expect good benefits, though, including paid time off, health care, retirement and savings programs, and even child-care centers.

**Sites to Check Out**
- **www.cia.gov**—The Central Intelligence Agency Web site. Here you can look up different careers, view current job openings, and create an application online.

- **www.cia.gov/kids-page/index.html**—The CIA Kid's Page is bizarre in its openness, but interesting.

- **http://federaljobs.net/ciajobs.htm**—Find job listings here.

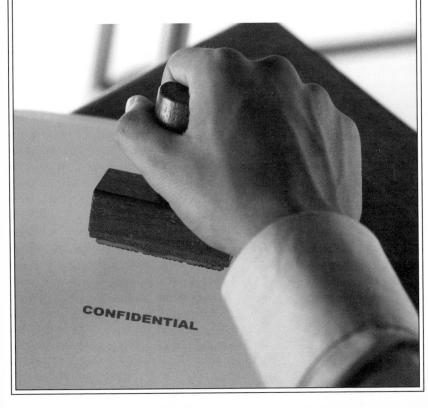

## Circus Performer

### What You Do

You might swing from a trapeze, balance on a tightrope, be catapulted through the air from a glorified seesaw, or perform any number of other impressive feats. If you're with a traveling circus, you'll spend a lot of time on the road between shows, likely moving from one city to another for months at a time. Most shows will be at night, but rehearsals will take up some of your daytime hours.

### Why It's Risky

This will, of course, depend on what your particular talent is. Acrobats will often experience stress injuries from performing the same movements over and over, and no matter how much you practice, there is still the possibility of falling, slipping, or being dropped. Performers who work with animals are more likely to be bitten, mauled, or stomped on, should their four-legged fellow performer become rebellious.

Circus Performer

### What You Need

Acrobats, contortionists, dancers, and trapeze artists often train from the time they're young children, working on the flexibility and strength they need to perform the stunts. Modern circuses may include acts by break dancers, trick bicyclists, or even divers. Basically, you need some sort of impressive skill that will wow the audiences.

### The Payoff

Highly skilled circus performers make between $40,000 and $70,000 a year. Room and board is often included for traveling circuses, too.

### Sites to Check Out

- **www.circuscenter.org**—This San Francisco school is one of the most famous for the circus arts.

- **www.circusnews.com**—This site offers a wealth of circus-related news and information.

- **www.circusguide.net**—Find tips for circus artists, watch videos of other performers for inspiration, and find jobs under the Circus Forum tab.

## Coast Guard

### What You Do

The Coast Guard's mission is "to protect the public, the environment, and the United States' economic and security interests in any maritime region in which those interests may be at risk, including international waters and America's coasts, ports, and inland waterways." So you may spend most of your time floating around the Statue of Liberty keeping an eye out for wayward tourists, or you might be jumping out of helicopters into raging seas to rescue victims of a shipwreck.

### Why It's Risky

Watch *The Guardian*. Or just picture yourself jumping into the ocean in the middle of the worst storm you can imagine (lightning, pounding rain, thrashing winds, waves bigger than your house) with nothing but flippers and a snorkel (okay, you can add a wet suit to the image—this isn't a kinky porn video). Now you have to climb into

Coast Guard

a sinking boat and rescue six fishermen single-handedly. Getting the idea? Yeah, it's risky.

**What You Need**

As the U.S. Coast Guard's Web site helpfully states, "If you are afraid of being in, on, or near the water, you are not eligible to apply." You'll do yourself a favor if you're good at swimming before you enlist for training, too. And then there are the basic requirements for entering any branch of the U.S. military: high school education or GED, U.S. citizenship, and you have to be between seventeen and twenty-seven years old for active duty.

**The Payoff**

You'll start off at around $1,250/month, plus a sign-on bonus (which can be quite substantial—currently up to $40,000), food, and clothing. So basically, what you make you keep, since all your expenses are covered. Visit the Coast Guard Web site for a current pay chart. You get excellent life insurance, too.

**Sites to Check Out**

- **www.uscg.mil**—The U.S. Coast Guard official Web site.

- **www.gocoastguard.com**—This site will answer most of your questions.

- **www.jacksjoint.com/seatales.htm**—Stories from people in the Coast Guard.

# Commercial Fishing Crew in Alaska

### What You Do

Catch salmon, crabs, halibut, or other fish, depending on the season, off the coast of Alaska. As a deckhand, you will be working irregular hours baiting hooks, lugging forty- to sixty-pound anchors, coiling heavy fishing line, and possibly hacking ice off the boat and washing down the decks.

### Why It's Risky

Commercial fishing in Alaska is recognized as one of the most hazardous jobs in the nation. In 1991, a Commercial Fishing Vessel Safety Act took effect, requiring boats to carry certain safety and survival instruments, but buoys and a life jacket are really no match for storms at sea. Still, when considering a job, be sure that safety precautions are being followed. Use common sense: If a boat looks cruddy and unkempt, think about whether its owner is the one

Commercial Fishing Crew in Alaska

you want to trust with your life. A sloppy boat may mean sloppy safety standards.

### What You Need

You must be able-bodied and a hard worker—this is a very physically demanding job. You should also be able to get along amicably with a crew, even when you're wet, cold, tired, and all stuck on a small boat for days at a time. You'll also want quality rain gear ($200 to $300) and a commercial fishing crew license ($175, or $60 if you are an Alaska resident). Plus, of course, however much it will cost to get yourself to Alaska.

### The Payoff

Deckhands usually make 1.5 percent to 10 percent of the adjusted gross catch (in other words, the more fish you haul out of the ocean, the more money you put in your pocket). Some boats offer a daily rate of $50 to $100 instead. Look online and you will find stories about novice crew hands earning $80,000 in eight months, but it's not likely you'll make more than $2,000 a month, if that. Accommodations are often provided as part of the deal, and you'll get to see one of the most beautiful states in the nation.

**Sites to Check Out**

- **www.labor.state.ak.us/esd_alaska_jobs/sea-food.htm**—The Alaska Department of Labor offers useful information and job listings.

- **www.admin.adfg.state.ak.us/license/**—The Alaska Department Fish and Game has information on obtaining a license.

- **www.alaskafishjobs.com**—An introduction to fishing jobs in Alaska. If you buy the book written by the author of the Web site, you'll get more comprehensive information.

- **www.alaska-summer-jobs.com**—This site includes details specific to various types of fishing.

## How You Get the Job

To get a position, most people wander up and down the docks talking to skippers and hoping someone else quits so they can take their place. Towns frequented by such hopefuls include Kodiak, Ketchikan, Homer, and Petersburg. Without experience to make you a more promising candidate for hire (and because living expenses in Alaska are high and you don't want to be stuck up there bumming around without a job for too long), you might be better off trying to secure a position before you go, using the resources listed here (or similar ones).

# Competitive Ballroom or Latin Dancer

### What You Do

Tango, waltz, foxtrot, quickstep, merengue, or otherwise dance with your partner around the ballroom floor. You'll be judged on technical criteria such as frame, posture, speed, timing, and body alignment. Women wear elaborate dresses, while men generally wear variations on a black tuxedo or tails.

### Why It's Risky

Think dancing is for sissies? Donna Shingler, who collided with a competitor during a high-speed spin mid-tango, might disagree. She was rushed to the hospital with a dislocated jaw-bone and a concussion. Injuries like this occur relatively frequently, not surprisingly when you consider there are generally eight couples at once flying around the floor at top speed, all more concerned with impressing the judges than watching their neighbors. Crashing into

Competetitve Ballroom or Latin Dancer

other couples is the most common hazard, but tricky lifts, flips, and slippery wooden floors can all lead to serious injury.

### What You Need
Most ballroom or Latin dancers train for several years before entering advanced competitions. Knowledge of the steps and the physical ability to execute them properly with a partner take time to attain. You may want a choreographer to help design your routine, and if you're not in proper attire, don't expect to win the judges' approval.

### The Payoff
First-place couples in professional competitions generally walk away with around $1,000 (so, $500 per person). Most dancers supplement their income with performing and/or teaching.

### Sites to Check Out
- **http://usadance.org**—"Promoting the quality & quantity of dance in the USA."

- **www.abcdresses.com**—Affordable ballroom competition dresses.

- **www.ballroomdancers.com**—An introduction to the world of ballroom dancing.

## Deep-Sea Fisherman

### What You Do

Fishermen generally work long hours, setting and dropping cages or nets (often with bait), pulling them up, then packing the fish on ice. They also keep busy cleaning the decks and possibly doing minor repairs to the ship.

### Why It's Risky

Shipwreck! Even if the ship doesn't get battered to pieces by a raging storm, there's the risk of losing your balance and falling overboard at any time. Or you could fall off the slippery gangways or ladders onto the deck (this might not kill you, but you'll have some serious bruises at the very least). Also, whenever there is electrical equipment used in the midst of an abundance of water, danger is not far away. And you never know when a shark is going to jump on board and take a bloody bite out of your arm (okay, maybe I'm letting my imagination go a bit here).

Deep-Sea Fisherman

### What You Need
Strength, an immunity to seasickness, and a willingness to work in windy, rainy, and possibly cold conditions.

### The Payoff
Once, off the coast of Japan, a 444-pound bluefin tuna was caught and sold for $173,600. But don't expect to hit the jackpot every day. If you work for a summer on a boat in Alaska, you might make anywhere from $5,000 to $15,000. Often your pay is a small percentage (around 1.5 percent) of the adjusted gross catch.

### Sites to Check Out
- **www.fishing-jobs.com**—"Definitive advice on commercial fishing jobs."

- **www.jobmonkey.com**—offers more job listings.

- **www.seafish.org**—This site is primarily about commercial fishing in the UK, but it has useful information for fishermen anywhere.

# Drug Enforcement Administration

**What You Do**

The DEA conducts investigations into foreign and domestic illegal drug activity and trafficking and tries to put a stop to them. As an agent, you'll set up surveillance, arrange undercover investigations, and strive to bring drug offenders to justice. If you get hired, you'll undergo sixteen weeks of Basic Agent Training, during which you'll learn to handle firearms, practice self-defense and arrest techniques, do a lot of push-ups and sit-ups, and study drugs.

**Why It's Risky**

Even when you're not in the middle of a bust, you'll likely have to hang out in places where violence is a way of life. And if the criminals know you're part of the DEA, you'll become a target. Recently, a forty-year-old supervisory special agent of the DEA was jumped, abducted, and beaten on his way from an organized-crime

Drug Enforcement Administration

drug-enforcement conference. He died from his wounds.

### What You Need

You must be between the ages of twenty-one and thirty-seven, pass psychological and polygraph tests, go through multiple in-depth interviews, and be reasonably physically fit. A criminal justice degree or past experience is helpful, as is knowing more than one language.

### The Payoff

Between $35,000 and $50,000/year depending on your experience and expertise.

### Sites to Check Out

- **www.usdoj.gov/dea/index.htm**—The DEA's official site.

- **www.criminaljusticedegreesguide.com/ jobs/deaagent.html**—A clear and concise overview of the job and how to get it.

# Electrician

### What You Do

As an electrician, you'll install and maintain the wires and fuses that allow electricity to flow to our homes and factories. The work involves a lot of hand and power tools—get familiar with a pair of pliers and a hacksaw. You'll also read a lot of blueprints and you'll need to comply with the National Electric Code as well as state and local building codes to ensure electrical safety.

### Why It's Risky

It's not too difficult to get electrocuted when you're working with live wires all day. Alternating current, which is typically what you'll be dealing with, has the nasty little habit of seizing your muscles. At fifteen milliamperes and above, you won't have the muscle control to let go of whatever is zapping you. At about twenty milliamps, ventricular fibrillation starts to occur, which is when your heart starts twitching uncontrollably. Soon your heart and lungs will stop, which means you're dead.

In addition to the dangers of electrical shock, you'll be working on ladders and lifting heavy objects, which means falls and back injuries are very real concerns. Also, you'd better be a good clotter, because you're gonna get cut. According to one apprentice electrician, "It's not a full day's work until you bleed."

### What You Need

To be a licensed electrician, the first step is an apprenticeship; expect four to five years of training, including at least 144 classroom hours

Electrician

and 2,000 on-the-job training hours. You've got to be at least eighteen, and probably have a high school diploma or GED. It'll help to be a math whiz and to have a solid grounding in practical physics, and to be handy with a power drill and knowledgeable about safety and first aid. And if you can't tell green from blue, forget about it. As an electrician, you need to be able to differentiate between a wire that's safe to touch and one that will make you crispy.

### The Payoff

Your pay will depend on your experience, your employer (if you're not self-employed), and whether or not you're a union member. Expect the median pay to be from $16 to $28 per hour, but the lowest 10 percent can make under $13 an hour, while the big dogs in the top 10 percent can make over $36 an hour.

### Sites to Check Out

- **www.bls.gov/oco/ocos206.htm**—The U.S. Department of Labor offers statistics on electricians and their jobs.

- **http://www.elec-toolbox.com**—For electricians and by electricians, this site offers formulae, tricks of the trade, and lots of other helpful information.

- **www.njatc.org**—Get started on your electrical career with help from the National Joint Apprenticeship and Training Committee.

## Elephant Trainer

**What You Do**

You might be training an elephant for life in the circus or zoo, for hauling and extracting logs from areas machines cannot access, or to become a farmhand, pulling plows or other farm machinery. (The latter two are more popular in Thailand than in the United States.) You will give the elephant rewards (usually food, such as apple slices) to encourage good behavior. You will probably also be responsible for helping the elephant to bathe, and possibly keeping his or her living area clean.

**Why It's Risky**

They're huge! We're talking 10,000 to 15,000 pounds. If he doesn't like the training regime you're imposing on him, he could squash you like an ant. Or just clobber you with an eighteen-inch-wide foot. Elephants can be very sweet and docile, but make one mad and you're done for.

Elephant Trainer

**What You Need**
Start with an affinity for large animals. A veterinarian degree or a certification in animal training will be a help. You may want to volunteer at a zoo or elephant-training facility to gain some experience and find out if a career in elephants is really for you.

**The Payoff**
$10 to $20/hour

**Sites to Check Out**

- **www.changthai.com**—An elephant conservation center in Thailand where you can pay to work alongside the mahouts (elephant trainers). A two-day course costs the equivalent of about $170 and includes food and accommodations. You may even get to visit the elephant dung paper factory.

- **www.animalschool.net**—Exotic-animal-training school in Santa Clarita, California.

- **www.elephants.se**—This site has a wealth of information about all things elephant related.

**EMT**

### What You Do

You're the first to provide medical attention when somebody needs it most, and you provide it while speeding toward a hospital in an ambulance with its sirens screaming. Expect to perform CPR, stop blood flow from wounds, and calm panicked victims. It'll be up to you to preserve a human life until hospital staff can take over. No pressure, though.

### Why It's Risky

As an EMT, you're exposed to a lot of blood, which puts you at risk of contracting HIV and other blood-borne illnesses. Also, patients don't always want to come quietly into your ambulance; sometimes you'll roll up to discover a coked-out stab victim brandishing a switchblade, or the loser of a gunfight packing heat and a serious attitude.

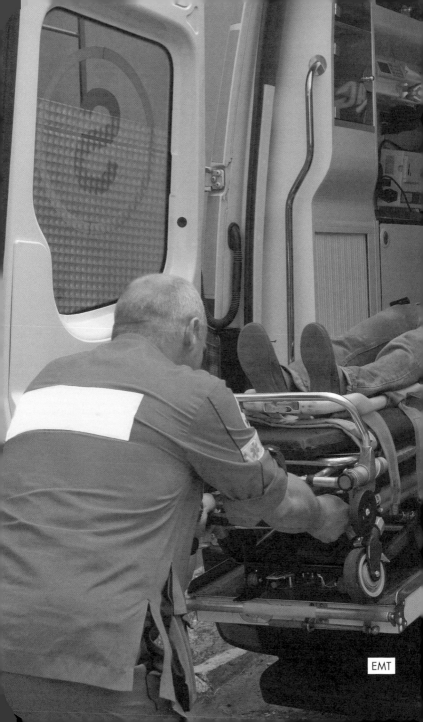

EMT

### What You Need

A driver's license, a high school diploma, and EMT certification, which you get by passing a written and practical examination. There are three levels of EMTs: Basic, Intermediate, and Paramedic. Each level requires a different amount of training, with paramedics requiring the most. Accordingly, paramedics are allowed to perform more invasive procedures than are basics or intermediates. EMTs are required to recertify every two years.

Physically, an EMT needs to be strong enough to lift patients smoothly and have sharp vision to avoid accidents on the road. You'll also need to keep your head under some serious pressure.

### The Payoff

EMT and paramedic salaries range from $18,000 to around $50,000.

### Sites to Check Out

- **www.nremt.org**—Find courses, get certified, and find a job here.

- **www.naemt.org/default.aspx**—The NAEMT represents and serves Emergency Medical Services personnel through advocacy, educational programs, and research.

- **www.emtb.com/9e**—Get help with those certification tests.

# Experimental Test Pilot

### What You Do

Test planes for safety and functionality before anyone else gets in the cockpit. According to Eric Volstad, a test pilot for the Canadian Air Force, "Experimental test pilots fly new and modified airplanes; occasionally fool around with nerdy calculus equations; and generally spend entirely too much time writing long, technical reports."

### Why It's Risky

You're testing an aircraft to see if it works. If it doesn't, well, here's hoping someone packed your parachute properly. In the 1950s and '60s, test pilots were dropping like flies; just about every week another pilot was killed. Today you have a much better chance of survival, but it's still considered the most dangerous form of peacetime piloting.

Experimental Test Pilot

### What You Need

First you'll need to be a pilot, and then you'll need another year of specialized training. An engineering degree is helpful, and it's definitely a plus if you're really quick at solving problems in high-pressure situations.

### The Payoff

$25,000–$200,000/year, depending on your level of experience and the company you work for. And if you're looking for a steady adrenaline supply, search no further.

### Sites to Check Out

- **www.testpilots.com**—One test pilot's description of his career.

- **www.avjobs.com**—Here you'll find details on the job, tips for interviewing, job listings, and more.

- **www.ntps.com**—The National Test Pilot School is one of about seven major test pilot schools in the world, and the only one specifically for civilians.

## Farmworker

### What You Do

This will, of course, depend on what kind of farm you're working on. There are dairy farms, chicken farms, horse farms, and don't forget worm farms. Then there are farms that concentrate on cultivating food crops. Within those categories there are certified organic farms, rotational grazers, corporate farms, family farms, and so on. Most farms actually do more than one thing (they might raise chickens and corn, for example). Whatever sort of farm you end up on, your job will almost undoubtedly include some heavy physical labor (shoveling manure, operating machinery, wrangling cattle, lugging bales of hay).

### Why It's Risky

Animals, machinery (especially when it's old), and weather (which you'll be exposed to regularly) are all unpredictable. You might get

Farmworker

kicked, crushed, or struck by lightning. In addition, chemicals used on nonorganic farms can cause asthma, eye irritation, or skin problems, and routine lifting or bad working postures can lead to injury.

### What You Need
Strength, determination, and a pair of overalls (okay, that last one's optional).

### The Payoff
$8–$15/hour. Plus the satisfaction that comes from fresh air and exercise. And probably a good night's sleep.

### Sites to Check Out
- **www.farmandranchjobs.com**—Find jobs, read articles about farming, and find links to other resources.

- **www.transitionsabroad.com**—If you're interested in working on a farm in another country, check out the Farm Jobs Abroad link under Short-Term Work.

## Firefighter

### What You Do

You will put out fires whenever they occur, often rescuing people who are trapped in them. You may work twenty-four-hour shifts, and your schedule will sometimes include weekends and major holidays. Most of the time you'll be doing fire prevention and inspection, teaching elementary schools kids how to "stop, drop, and roll," and lecturing teens who pulled the fire alarm to get out of a test.

### Why It's Risky

Fire kills more people every year than any other natural force. A building on fire loses structural integrity every minute and many firefighters perish due to a collapsed roof or floor or blocked exit. Your day-to-day heroic acts take a toll on your body, with carbon monoxide and smoke inhalation, burns, and potentially, cardiovascular disease. Firefighters usually have

Firefighter

poor heart health due to exposure to substances that prevent transport of oxygen in the blood and hypertension caused by stress and strenuous exercise. If that weren't enough, 25 percent of U.S. firefighter fatalities are caused by vehicle whoa! accidents when traveling to and from fires.

### What You Need
You need to be at least eighteen years old, have a high school diploma, and train at a state-approved fire academy. Courage and a desire to help your community will help you get through those forty-two- to fifty-six-hour workweeks.

### The Payoff
Pay is determined by rank and location. You can make between $20,000 and $66,000/year, with higher ranks such as captain and fire chief earning up to $100,000. "Location, location, location" doesn't just apply to real estate: a Chicago suburb firefighter will have a base salary of $51,000 while one from a town in Wyoming is more likely to have a base of around $19,100. To get an accurate record of salaries in your area, visit your city or town hall.

### Sites to Check Out
• **www.usfa.dhs.gov/index.shtm**—The United States Fire Administration Web site.

- **www.firehouse.com**—The Web site companion to *Firehouse* magazine, featuring articles about disasters and brave rescues, training videos, and job posts.

- **www.firefighter.com**—The place to go for firefighter paraphernalia, from T-shirts and hoodies to EMS rescue equipment.

## Lingo

*Jake*—A New England term for a firefighter.
*Kelly Day* refers to a Chicago mayor named Kelly who gave firefighters a day of rest as part of their work cycle.
*PPE*—Personal Protection Equipment.

## Hazmat Diver

### What You Do

Dive into sewers, nuclear reactors, or toxic spills to fix clogs, recover lost bodies or objects, suck out waste, or maintain equipment. You'll wear a full-body suit with thick gloves, a helmet, mask, and boots, all of which are kept pressurized to help prevent contaminated liquids from seeping in should your suit be punctured. Sewer diving is often considered the most dangerous form of hazmat diving. Not only is raw sewage full of disease, but syringes and broken glass often make their way into sewers, just waiting to rip open your protective gear. It's pretty crappy—literally.

### Why It's Risky

There's a reason they call these materials hazardous. Hazardous wastes by definition contain carcinogenic, mutagenic, or teratogenic compounds; are radioactive; catch fire or explode easily; or are capable of corroding metal containers. That's the stuff you'll be swimming

Hazmat Diver

around in. Saturation divers are saturated with gas so that they can stay underwater at great depths for extended periods for weeks at a time. The decompression from these dives can take a month and cause a great deal of wear and tear on your brain. A saturation diver can only work for around three years until they have to stop or sustain serious brain damage.

### What You Need
You'll need training and experience in diving, chemistry, and knowledge of hazardous materials. Take a commercial diving training course (around $10,000, but you'll make it back fairly quickly once you land a job). You'll need up-to-date vaccinations against tetanus and hepatitis.

### The Payoff
$3,500 to $4,000/month.

### Sites to Check Out
- **www.hazmatdiving.com**—Don't be dissuaded by the German on this Web site; just scroll down for the English translation. You'll find pictures of diver equipment and divers in action.

- **www.diversacademy.com**—One school offering commercial diving courses.

- **www.advanceddiving.com**—This could be your future employer!

## Human Cannonball

**What You Do**

Climb into the barrel of a cannon and hang out until you're blasted above the thundering crowds, soaring through the air, and land (hopefully) in a net, inflated bag, or big pool. The first human to be shot from a cannon and land in a net some distance away was a fourteen-year-old girl who flew across the Royal Aquarium in London in 1877. It was a fantastic act—that is, until the time she missed the net and broke her back. She spent the rest of her days in a steel corset. Since then, cannonball stunts have gotten more and more incredible. The current world record is held by David "Cannonball" Smith, Jr., who, in 2002 was propelled 201 feet, traveling at around 90 miles per hour.

**Why It's Risky**

The cannons you'll be shot out of actually use compressed air rather than gunpowder, or else it would be a one-time job and rather gruesome.

Human Cannonball

Thus, the danger is neither in the launch nor the flight—it's in the landing. According to one recent count, out of approximately fifty human cannonballs, thirty have been killed as a result of crashing outside of the net. It is also common to black out during the flight (probably from overdosing on adrenaline). Again, it's not a problem while you're in the air, but executing a proper landing while you're unconscious requires more than your average bit of luck.

### What You Need
A cannon, a lot of compressed air, a huge net, airbag, or pool, and a hearty dose of bravado.

### The Payoff
If you do your stunt for the circus, expect to make $40,000 to $70,000 a year. If it's your own traveling show that you perform at events or celebrations, you set your own price depending on your area. Chances are there won't be a lot of competition, so you can make a pretty penny. Just remember to account for the cost of the cannon, air compressor, and insurance.

### Sites to Check Out
- **www.cannon-mania.com/human-cannon. htm**—Read the history of human cannonballs and see an assortment of old photos of folks being blasted through the air.

- **www.humancannonball.us/index.html**—David "the Cannon" Smith, Jr.'s personal site.

- **www.aircompressorsdirect.com**—You'll need an air compressor. Start shopping here.

Photo by Michael Palumbo

# Human Crash Test Dummy

**What You Do**

Plastic crash test dummies have done a lot to improve the safety of vehicles, but when it comes right down to it, they show you what happens to plastic—not a human skull—when it meets a glass windshield. Humans react to an impending crash in ways that a dummy can't, by tensing their muscles, for instance, which changes the effects of the crash on their bodies. As a human crash test dummy, you'll drive into brick walls, wham your knee repeatedly into a metal bar, or allow a twenty-pound pendulum to swing into your chest, with the goal of demonstrating what a car crash will do to a human body.

**Why It's Risky**

You will, at the very least, be sore after a crash. The conditions are controlled in such a way that you should not be seriously injured or killed,

Human Crash Test Dummy

but when you're talking about slamming head-on into concrete or spinning into another moving object, there are no safety guarantees.

**What You Need**

A driver's license, guts, and a willingness to abuse your body on a regular basis.

**The Payoff**

Here's the bad news. Most human crash test dummies are volunteers. And the human crash test dummy heyday seems to have been in the sixties and seventies. However, you sadomasochists out there, don't despair! Surely there's a shortage of dummy volunteers. Why not start your own human crash test dummy business? Call up Ford and offer your services. Considering that a plastic crash test dummy costs around $150,000, you—a thinking, feeling (though possibly crazy) human being—ought to be able to pull down a solid six-figure salary no problem. Let me know how it goes.

**Sites to Check Out**

• **www.crashtestdummyolympics.co.uk**—Get some practice here to hone your crashing skills.

- **www.ford.com**—Did you practice on the Web site above? Good. Now give Ford a call.

- **http://www.salon.com/health/col/roac/ 1999/11/19/crash_test**—If you have patience enough to type in this long url you'll be rewarded with an article about Professor Lawrence M. Patrick, who was a human crash test dummy for fifteen years.

### Inspiration

"Too many people are thinking of security instead of opportunity. They seem to be more afraid of life than death."

—**James F. Bymes**

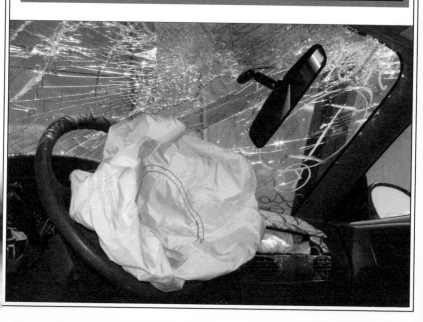

## Laboratory/Medical Technician

**What You Do**

Medical technologists test samples of body fluids (blood, urine, bone marrow, semen, etc.) for disease and abnormalities. Lab techs don't necessarily work in the health industry, but can take part in research or testing. This could involve a variety of tasks, including taking samples from animals. You could work at a hospital, private lab, or university.

**Why It's Risky**

You'll be exposed to dangerous chemicals and diseases, the biggest threat being HIV/AIDS. (Granted, these dangers are minimized when safety precautions are met, such as wearing the proper gear, tightening a lid, or disposing of needles correctly.) You're also at risk for carpal tunnel syndrome, repetitive motion injuries (RMIs), varicose veins, and other work-related conditions.

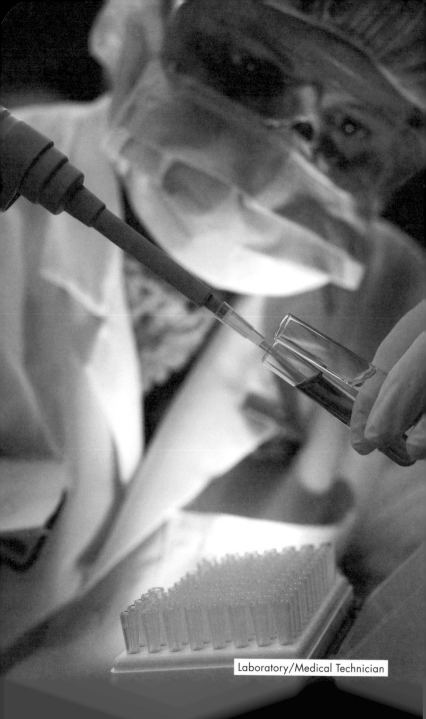
Laboratory/Medical Technician

## What You Need

You'll need a bachelor's degree in medical technology or a science such as biology or chemistry. Most four-year programs are three years on campus, one year in the field. Your year of clinical rotations will help you decide which area to specialize in. You can choose from automated chemistry, cytology, cytogenetics, hematology, microbiology, molecular biology, immunology, histology, or toxicology. You'll need an ASCP (American Society of Clinical Pathologists) certification, and about a dozen states require a license.

## The Payoff

The median salary for an ASCP certified technologist is just over $55,000 a year. A large shortage of MTs is predicted for the next decade, due to a decrease in education programs, an increase in retirees, and the growing number of people needing health care. So you can expect very little competition getting a job and probably incentives to stay.

One of the best parts of being a medical or laboratory tech is the variety of schedules. As doctors need results at all times of the day, there are usually three shifts spread over twenty-four hours. Some institutions offer four ten-hour days instead of the usual five days of eight hours each.

**Sites to Check Out**

- **www.allalliedhealthschools.com/featured/ medical-lab-tech**—A guide to MT programs by state

- **www.labtechnicianjobs.com**—Find jobs here.

- **www.mshealthcareers.com/careers/med- labtech.htm**—Learn more about lab techs and other medical careers here.

## Lion Tamer

**What you do**

Taming a lion is not much different than training a dog or any other kind of animal. Except that lions are often over five hundred pounds and will instinctively tear you apart with their teeth and claws if they don't like your technique. But still, the main tenets of animal training are the same whether you're dealing with a golden retriever pup or Scar from *The Lion King*. You'll use toys, treats, verbal reinforcement, and possibly—should your furry friend get too frisky—a fire extinguisher to encourage proper manners. It's easiest to start when the lion is a cub, mostly because their jaws are a lot smaller and you'll be more likely to get a big scratch than to lose your head if things go wrong. With patience, perseverance, and a little luck, you may be able to teach a lion to do all kinds of entertaining tricks. And if the training is done properly and with the right attitude, he

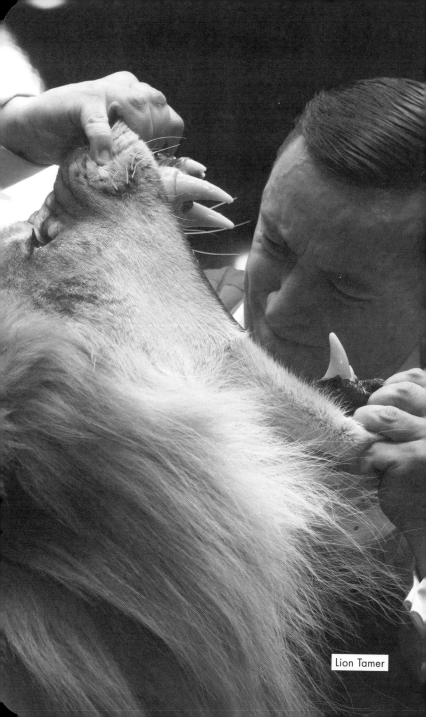

Lion Tamer

or she will enjoy the tricks as much as the audience does. You'll probably also need to do the more boring animal-care stuff, like feeding and exercising the beasts, as well as watching for illnesses and getting your charges veterinary treatment when necessary.

### Why It's Risky

Have you ever been scratched by a house cat? If so, you probably know that cats are almost eerily quick, impulsive, moody, and capable of inflicting serious pain on another creature, often for no obvious reason. Lions can be very social, even very sweet, but if you rub them the wrong way you could end up as a snack.

### What You Need

Start off by volunteering at lion-rescue facilities, at the zoo, wild-animal park, or at a shelter. You may want to consider getting a degree in zoology or veterinary medicine and to try an internship where you can apply your learned skills. You should love big scary carnivores and be willing to suffer a few scratches on your way to lion-taming success.

### The Payoff

$10 to $50 an hour, depending on your level of expertise.

**Sites to Check Out**

- **www.wildthingsinc.com**—This California ranch is an animal sanctuary that offers opportunities to hang out with lions, intern, or take animal-training courses.

- **www.animalschool.net**—Another California exotic-animal training school.

- **www.aza.org**—The Association of Zoos and Aquariums.

## Lumberjack

### What You Do

Use saws and heavy equipment to cut down and delimb trees and possibly help transport them to a wood mill.

### Why It's Risky

Many sources deem logging the most dangerous industry in the United States. The reasons are fairly obvious, but I'll list them anyway. Chain saws are made for cutting wood, but are equally or more effective in cutting flesh. Trees are heavy and they don't get any lighter when they fall on top of you. Loggers often work in adverse weather conditions, too, and icy or slippery wet ground makes an already risky outdoor job even more dangerous.

### What You Need

Most loggers learn the trade by doing it, not through any sort of formal education. You will

Lumberjack

need to be able-bodied and willing to work out-doors in a wide range of weather conditions.

**The Payoff**
Lots of fresh air and about $15/hour.

**Sites to Check Out**
- **www.dnr.state.md.us/forests/gloss.html**—A useful list of forestry terms.

- **www.bls.gov/oco/ocos178.htm**—A thorough explanation of logging from the U.S. government's *Occupational Outlook Handbook*.

- **www.forestryusa.com**—Lots of forestry resources, including job listings.

**Inspiration**

"Ultimately we know deeply that the other side of every fear is a freedom."

**—Marilyn Ferguson**

# Meatpacker

**What You Do**

You kill 'em, so we can grill 'em. Meatpackers' tasks include everything from killing to skinning to butchering. You'll be hoisting massive heifer carcasses, walking on blood-slippery floors over dangerous machinery, and performing repetitive tasks that could damage your muscles in the long term. That's not even mentioning the exposure to dangerous chemicals (like ammonia) and bacteria (like E. coli).

**Why It's Risky**

Amputation is always a very real concern, as you'll be surrounded by machines such as the Meat Grinder, the Hide Puller, the Stun Gun, and, my personal favorite, the Gut Cooker. It's grueling work, and you've always got to be aware of your immediate surroundings, lest you get a meat hook to the eye. Slippery floors are likely to cause falls, which could be extra bad if you're carrying something heavy or sharp.

Meatpacker

Among the most serious and overlooked dangers of the meatpacking industry are cumulative trauma injuries, or those you get from doing the same motion over and over for hours every day. This can lead to carpal tunnel syndrome, trigger finger, or supraspinatus tendonitis.

Add to all that the stress factor when the line keeps speeding up and your buddies are crammed in side by side next to you, becoming less and less careful with their seriously sharp knives. Oh, and you might not want to make a snide comment to those coworkers—in 2000, 129 workers died on the job as a result of workplace violence.

**What You Need**
A strong stomach, lots of muscles, and a high tolerance for pain.

**The Payoff**
$7.50–$13 an hour.

**Sites to Check Out**
- **www.bls.gov/oes/current/oes513023.htm#ind**—The hard facts on slaughterhouse/meatpacking employment and pay.

- **www.ers.usda.gov/Publications/AER785**—Download a free publication on consolidation in the meatpacking industry.

# Mercenary

### What You Do

Consider yourself a rent-a-soldier. These days the term is "private military contractor," but the job is the same—you'll take part in military conflict not because of your patriotic convictions or because your country requires your service, but just for the cash. Needless to say, this is the most ruthless of dangerous jobs. You will work in a *very* dangerous environment, by yourself or with a team.

### Why It's Risky

War is dangerous for any soldier, but in many ways it's worse for a mercenary. You may find that your fellow soldiers treat you with less respect (if they know that you're a mercenary); if there's a choice between saving you and the pal they went to basic training with, guess who's going to be rotting on the battlefield? And don't expect to become a military hero. If you're

Mercenary

captured and discovered to be a mercenary, you'll be tried as a common criminal.

**What You Need**

Foremost, you have to have the right personality and mind-set to be a mercenary. If you easily crack under pressure, this is not the job for you. You must be decisive, quick thinking, and able to take a life without thinking twice. Physically, you should be strong and athletic; your health directly affects your performance and thus, your lifespan.

Blackwater Worldwide, a well-known security services company owned by a former Navy SEAL, looks for "qualified, skilled, [and] trustworthy" applicants. The reputable companies consider you "qualified" if you have military experience. You can be hired without military experience, but your team will probably be just as inexperienced as you are. . . . It's much safer to get the experience and work for a better company. As for being "skilled," this means not just knowing how to load a gun, but being an excellent marksman. Don't expect much on-the-job training; they're paying you because you're an expert, not because you want to become one. Also, the more assignments you go on, the more secrets you will have to keep. Confidentiality agreements are usually a part of the contract, so start thinking of good excuses for being gone for weeks at a time.

### The Payoff

It's well known that mercs are well paid, but because of the nature of the job it's very difficult to determine an average salary. In his book *Big Boy Rules,* Pulitzer Prize–winning reporter Steve Fainaru says the men he follows make $7,000/month. He also states that this is considered "underpaid" by contractors from other companies.

### Sites to Check Out

- **www.nrahq.org/shootingrange/findlocal. asp**—The National Rifle Association's guide to shooting ranges by state. You'll need somewhere to practice, plus you might make some gun-loving buddies.

- **www.proshieldint.com**—An employment agency for experienced military soldiers looking to enter the field of elite private security.

- **www.privatemilitary.org/home.html**— A Web site for mercenaries, with regularly updated news, articles, and links for private military contractors and companies.

## Metalworker

### What You Do

Working with metal is somewhat mythical, evoking images of Prometheus and the forming of armor and swords. It is so vital to human history that we've named prehistoric periods after our use of metals, the Bronze and Iron Ages. As a metalworker, you'll be forming, cutting, and joining metal, but probably not making a suit of armor, even though that would be really cool.

### Why It's Risky

There are a lot of opportunities for injury in metalworking, including heavy machinery, sharp tools, molten metal, and possible chemical and asbestos exposure. Most metalworkers work in factories, and although there are federal guidelines and inspections for your safety, accidents happen. You could be manufacturing parts of an airplane or creating large pieces of sheet metal to be used in construction. All that machinery

Metalworker

creates a very high noise level, which can lead to hearing loss. One of the most dangerous parts of metalworking is extracting the metal from ore, a mineral-bearing rock, with heat or some other process. Other metals and chemicals are released that can cause kidney, liver, bone, and blood damage over time.

### What You Need

You'll need a high school diploma, where your training might begin with classes like geometry and shop. Most metalworkers either attend a trade school, have a formal apprenticeship, or get on-the-job training. An apprenticeship takes from four to five years to finish, roughly the same time it would take you to become proficient through other training. Computer technology is now widespread in metalworking and your employer might train you on the programs or machines they use.

### The Payoff

The salary range for a metalworker is $36,000 to $50,000 a year. Apprentices normally start out at 40 to 50 percent of the pay for experienced employees, then work their way up.

### Sites to Check Out

- **www.bls.gov/oco/ocos214.htm**—"How to Become a Sheet Metal Worker" by the U.S. Department of Labor.

- **www.nmri.go.jp/eng/khirata/metalwork/index_e.html**—A beginner's guide to metalworking translated into English from Japanese. Some of the wording is a little off, but the instructions and numerous photographs are great.

- **www.asbestos.net/occupations/sheet-metal-worker.html**—An article evaluating metalworkers' exposure to asbestos.

**Miner**

**What You Do**

This will depend somewhat on what material you're mining. You might use heavy-duty machinery to clear away large piles of rock and debris or you might just use a shovel and a pick like miners have been for generations. Chances are you'll be working underground, often in cramped spaces.

**Why It's Risky**

You may be exposed to underground gases (which can ignite if so much as a tiny spark is present), and there are numerous instances of shafts failing, causing mines to collapse with the miners still inside. You may remember in August 2007 when six coal miners were trapped in a mine three miles from the entrance and 1,500 feet underground. These tragedies are less common than they used to be due to stricter regulations, but they still occur.

Miner

## What You Need

Some companies only require that you be physically fit and willing to work. With more recent advances in mining technology, some companies may want you to have a high school degree from a vocational school, or to have some other mining training.

## The Payoff

$40,000–$100,000/year. Yes, I know that's a wide range, but it depends on where you're mining, what you're mining, and whether you have any special knowledge or experience.

## Sites to Check Out

- **www.mining.com**—Everything mining related.

- **www.infomine.com/careers**—Find mining jobs around the world.

- **www.worldcoal.org**—Learn about coal mining here.

## Motocross Driver

**What You Do**

Motocross, if you haven't figured it out yet, is a combination of "motorcycle" and "cross country." As a motocross driver, you'll compete for prize money in one of the several varieties of motocross, like Supercross, Arenacross, Freestyle, and the less popular Supermoto. When you're not getting muddy on the course you'll be training, and possibly instructing to augment your income.

**Why It's Risky**

Imagine trying to control a bike that weighs 200 or more pounds on rocky, muddy, intentionally difficult terrain at speeds that would normally get you your license suspended. It's a recipe for disaster (and there are plenty of clips on YouTube to prove it if you don't believe me). Freestyle motocross, or FMX, has become very popular in recent years and the

Motocross Driver

jaw-dropping acrobatics freestylers perform create even more opportunities for injury. Bruises and broken bones are a part of the job, but a particularly bad collision could leave you paralyzed or headed to the grave.

**What You Need**

It takes skill, great balance, and guts to do motocross. Your first order of business is to buy a motocross bike. You'll also need a helmet and a racing jacket, which, besides looking really cool, actually has protective padding. The only way to get to the professional level is to practice (a lot) and take lessons. Motocross is an expensive hobby, though once you go pro you'll probably be sponsored, which means you'll get all your fancy clothes and equipment (plastered with your sponsor's name all over it) for free. A new bike will cost you $3,000 to $8,000, a helmet $80 to $500, a jacket $100 to $200, chest and back armor $50 to $100, plus gloves, goggles, boots.

**The Payoff**

Your only way to make a living as a motocross driver is to win and get prize money. As you make a name for yourself you can make more money with endorsement deals. The Motocross World Championship series takes place mostly in Europe, sometimes with "flyaway" rounds in places like Chile or Japan. The AMA American

National Championship consists of twelve rounds that take place across the United States. If you do freestyle motocross, you can tryout for the X Games. Yet the combined prize money won by the top thirty-five earnings leaders in 2006 (as listed in *Motocross Illustrated*) comes to about $2.35 million. Compared to other dangerous sports, that's not a lot of dough. However, there are other perks. Male or female, you'll probably find that telling members of the opposite sex you're a motocross driver will garner all sorts of attention.

### Sites to Check Out

- **www.amaproracing.com**—The American Motorcyclist Association Web site.

- **www.motorcycle-superstore.com**—An online store with a wide selection that will get you set up with everything except a bike.

- **www.motocross.com**—Find videos, photos, interviews with motocross drivers, and more here.

# Nuclear Plant Security Guard

**What You Do**

You will protect the facility from any vandals or thieves. This includes inspecting vehicles entering and leaving the plant, maintaining restricted areas, and evacuating personnel in emergency situations.

**Why It's Risky**

Two words: nuclear meltdown. The Chernobyl disaster remains to this day a horrifying "worst-case scenario," producing *four hundred* times more fallout than the bombing of Hiroshima. Health concerns aside, there are plenty of people to whom nuclear material is either repugnant or enticing. Anti-nuclear power activists might raid or vandalize the facility, and terrorists could attempt to get their hands on nuclear material or blueprints, or simply want to cause some serious damage. You don't take an oath to put the safety of others before your own like

Nuclear Plant Security Guard

cops do, but do you really want to be the person responsible for letting terrorists get weapons-grade uranium? Didn't think so. However, any sensible terrorist is going to make sure their job is done decisively and thoroughly by dropping a bomb or crashing a plane into the plant, at which point there's really nothing you can do except maybe pray, if there's time for that. Another thing to keep in mind: If you work at a nuclear plant, chances are you and your family live nearby, putting them at risk as well.

### What You Need

You must be at least eighteen years old. Most states require a license, known as your "guard card," acquired through training. Before you get your license, ask if your employer pays for the training or offers an installment plan to be taken out of your paycheck. Policies vary from company to company, but expect to have a drug screen and background check. You'll need additional training to carry a firearm.

### The Payoff

Expect $13.50–$17.50/hour to start at a security company, and $25–$50/hour working in-house as a "proprietary guard." You'll probably get health benefits, as well as overtime and holiday pay.

**Sites to Check Out**

- **www.nrc.gov**—The United States Nuclear Regulatory Commission Web site has lots of information on nuclear reactors, materials, and waste. They have fact sheets called Security Spotlights on topics like "Protecting Against Aircraft" and "Securing [Hazardous] Materials."

- **www.globalsecurity.org/military/library/ report/crs/rs21131.pdf**—This government document details the risk that nuclear plants face in being targeted for terrorism, as well as the countermeasures they must employ.

- **http://nnsa.energy.gov/index.htm**—The National Nuclear Security Administration is the Department of Energy's answer to growing concerns about the safety and security of the nuclear plants across the country. Their Web site contains useful news links and articles about the future of nuclear safety.

## Nursing Aide

### What You Do

There are numerous names for this job: nurse assistant, geriatric aide, orderly, hospital attendant. You will work at a hospital or nursing home as the patients' most frequent helper. This could include helping them eat, dress, bathe, get out of bed, and walk around. You'll answer when buzzed, make beds, take vital signs and record them, and report back to physicians.

### Why It's Risky

You'll be exposed to harsh chemicals and diseases, the biggest threat being HIV/AIDS. Your patients might be disoriented or violent, and if their doctor needs help, you'll be the one restraining the patient. There are plenty of aides who have gotten kicked or bitten over the years. You're also at risk for repetitive motion injuries (RMIs), varicose veins, back problems, and other work-related conditions. In addition,

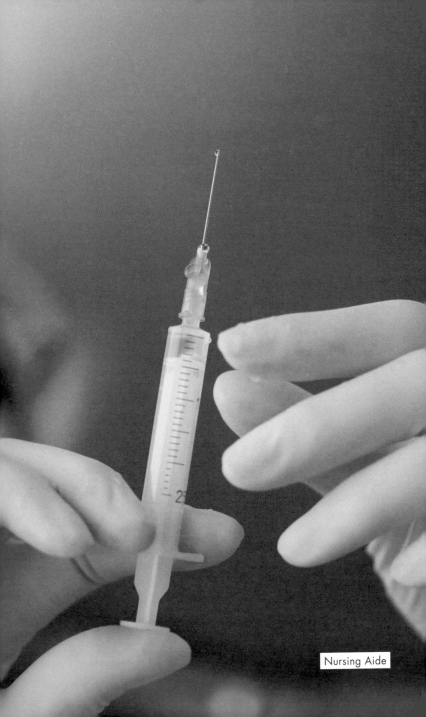
Nursing Aide

you'll be exposed to colds and viruses that frequently spread like wildfire through the tight quarters.

### What You Need
In most cases you need a high school diploma or GED. Then you'll need to enroll at a vocational school or community college. You'll take classes that will prepare you to care for patients, but most of the training will occur on the job as each institution has its own protocol and standards you must follow.

A nursing aide needs infinite patience, a desire to help others, and the drive to go the extra mile, because sometimes finding that different flavor of Jell-O can really make a difference. Even when the patient might not be aware of all that you're doing for them, their family certainly appreciates it.

### The Payoff
The Bureau of Labor Statistics sums it up quite well: "This occupation is characterized by modest entry requirements, low pay, high physical and emotional demands, and limited advancement opportunities." The median hourly wage in 2006 was $10.67, meaning 50 percent earned more and 50 percent earned *less* than that amount. Which means you could be cleaning out bedpans, feeding patients, and being on your

feet all day making just over minimum wage. If you wanted to move up you would have to get a bachelor's degree and pass the board exams to be a registered nurse. This is definitely one of those jobs where you have to do it because you love it, not for the money.

**Sites to Check Out**

- **www.nurselinkup.com**—Nurse LinkUp is an online community for registered nurses, but the content and focus is equally appropriate for a nursing aide. There are blogs, forums, and job postings that can be accessed after signing up.

- **www.medicalnewstoday.com/sections/ nursing**—*Medical News Today* has great articles that will keep you up-to-date with the latest news and research.

- **www.ncbi.nlm.nih.gov/sites/entrez**— PubMed, a service of the U.S. National Library of Medicine and the National Institute of Health, provides access to citations from biomedical literature and links to full documents.

## Oil Well Firefighter

### What You Do

If climbing into flame-engulfed buildings to rescue burning victims is not exciting enough for you, maybe you should consider becoming an oil well firefighter. Bigger fires, more smoke, high winds, chemicals in the air from burning crude oils . . . This is danger at its best. You may even get to use dynamite to "blow out" the fuel and oxygen feeding the flames. You'll use incredible amounts of water, specially equipped bulldozers, and maybe machine guns or dry chemicals to try to quell the fires, which sometimes last for months.

### Why It's Risky

Fire is dangerous. Fire fed by millions of dollars' worth of oil is *really* dangerous. Myron Kinley, who died in 1978, was a dedicated oil well firefighter who lost his brother in a blast of well gas, had a permanently crippled leg from

Oil Well Firefighter

an accident with machinery on the job, was covered with scars, and once spent five weeks on his stomach in a hospital recovering from scorching flames blown suddenly his way.

 **What You Need**
Fearless determination. Seriously! Another pioneer in the field, Red Adair, says in his biography: "I'd keep walking, not knowing exactly what was happening at the wellhead or on the floor of the drilling rig 'cause you never know until you're there and I'd say, 'I will defeat it, whatever it is. I will win.' But that's a lonely walk, boy, you better believe it."

But it's not recommended to battle flaming oil rigs with guts alone. You must be a trained and certified firefighter, with experience in engineering and explosives a plus (some capping strategies involve blowing up the well). The usual career path is a few years of standard firefighting, followed by specialized oil well training. You'll learn the unique techniques and technology to battle everything from marine, offshore drilling fires to widespread ones in a hostile area (like the 1991 Kuwaiti fires at the end of the Gulf War). In the United States, the Texas Engineering Extension Service (TEEX) at Texas A&M University is considered the best program in the country. TEEX is also home to the National Emergency Response and Rescue Training Center, so you're in good company.

### The Payoff
While getting your experience with standard firefighting, you can make between $20,000 and $66,000 year, depending on where you live and your rank. In general, cities pay better because they have a larger budget. As an oil well specialist you'll start at around $50,000 a year and can work your way up to $100,000 and more.

### Sites to Check Out
- **http://oilrigjobs.calvinmarketing.com/blog/jobs-in-oil-field**—Find jobs here.

- **www.safetyboss.net/mainpage.html**—Web site of Safety Boss, a blowout company based in Canada.

- **http://query.nytimes.com/gst/fullpage.html?res=9A04E5DA113CF93AA3575BC0A9629C8B63stm**—Apologies for the long URL, but this is the obituary of Paul "Red" Adair, a legendary oil well firefighter. (John Wayne plays a character based on Red in the movie *Hellfighters*.) He founded Red Adair Company Inc., an oil fire and blowout task force that quells an average of forty-two fires a year.

# Paratrooper

### What You Do

You'll operate as part of an airborne military force, jumping out of airplanes into enemy territory. Some areas cannot be reached by ground due to the geography or enemy defenses. Paratroopers have the unique advantage of being able to drop out of the sky from anywhere at any time.

### Why It's Risky

Add to the usual dangers of battle (getting shot or blown up, for instance) the risk of falling hundreds of feet. One would hope that your parachute will open properly and do its job, but a big black balloon floating in the sky is also a good target, and it's not easy to steer a parachute out of a bullet's path. High winds can cause paratroopers to be blown off course, possibly separating you from the rest of your

Paratrooper

unit, getting you tangled in the lines of a fellow troop, or landing you in a tree.

### What You Need

Besides the basic requirements for entering any branch of active military duty for the United States (high school education or GED, U.S. citizenship, and being between the ages of seventeen and twenty-seven), you'll need to undergo at least three weeks of special training in Fort Benning, Georgia. There you'll practice landings, exiting aircrafts, and proper parachute safety (is that an oxymoron?).

### The Payoff

As with all military branches, you'll start off at around $1,250/month. But don't forget sign-on bonuses (which can be up to $40,000), food, and sometimes clothing. So basically, what you make you keep, since virtually all your expenses will be covered. And if you decide the military isn't for you, you can always use that training to work as a skydiving instructor.

### Sites to Check Out

- **www.paratrooper.net**—This site advertises itself as a "wellspring of knowledge and unending witty commentary regarding the airborne community."

- **www.geocities.com/raymondrjs/armypar-achuting.html**—Memoirs of a paratrooper, with a surprisingly cheerful slant.

- **www.armyparatrooper.org**—Create a free account on this site to look at photos, join discussions with current paratroopers, and read blogs from other members.

## Plumber

### What You Do

This job dates back to the Roman Empire, when the Roman baths used pipes made of lead, or *plumbum* in Latin. An expert with the material was known as a *plumbarius*, which turned into the modern "plumber." You'll unclog, repair, and install pipes and plumbing systems in homes and commercial areas.

### Why It's Risky

Pipelayers and plumbers are liable to fall from ladders, get cuts from sharp metal edges or tools, or suffer burns from hot pipes and welding equipment. There is also a risk of asbestos exposure and lead paint poisoning while installing pipes in old walls. Plus, there are plenty of nasty things that can be inside pipes (human waste, dead animals, condoms, etc.) that could make you sick.

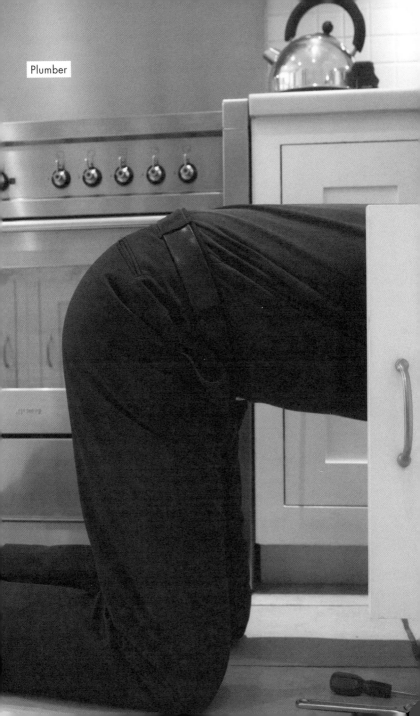

Plumber

## What You Need

Plumbing codes are strict because of the health problems that arise from not having potable hot and cold water or proper sewage removal. As such, you should first find out what the licensing requirements are for your area. You'll need to attend a trade school, apprentice to a master plumber, or apply for a union four-year program. One out of twenty applicants gets into the program, and if you make it, you'll complete about 2,000 hours of on-the-job training and about 200 hours in the classroom. Whichever route you take, you'll learn drafting and blueprint reading, basic mathematics, applied physics, chemistry, and local codes and regulations.

## The Payoff

Plumbers and pipelayers have one of the highest-paying construction jobs. The average hourly wage for plumbers is around $20, with the highest 10 percent earning closer to $35 an hour.

## Sites to Check Out

- **www.ua.org**—The United Association of Journeymen and Apprentices of the Plumbing and Pipefitting Industry of the United States and Canada, who thankfully go by just "UA," have a Web site that is a great resource for future plumbers.

- **www.plumbingagent.com**—Find jobs here.

- **www.theplumber.com**—This site has a wealth of plumbing advice.

## Police Officer

### What You Do

Prevent and stop crime, respond to emergency situations, and keep the peace. You can work a traditional "beat" or be a part of a special unit like SWAT, K9, Special Operations, Narcotics, or Crime Scene Investigation.

### Why It's Risky

Murderers, thieves, rapists—you'll be the enemy of the most dangerous people around. And rather than staying out of their way, you'll be expected to confront them. In 2007, 186 officers were killed on the job. In the near future, crime is expected to escalate, due to the economic crisis. While the level of risk varies for different kinds of police and their respective duties, even the cop standing on the corner directing traffic has a pretty good chance of getting hit by an angry (or spacey) motorist.

Police Officer

## What You Need

A bachelor's degree in political science, criminal justice, psychology, or other related field is recommended. It will give you an edge over fellow applicants and can lead to better starting pay and career advancement. You'll have to be in great shape, simply because you can't catch bad guys if you can't, well, catch up. After applying to your local police academy, be prepared for a drug test, background check, lie-detector test, fitness exam, and finally, an interview with a psychologist.

## The Payoff

Police and sheriff's patrol officers had median annual earnings of $47,460 in 2006. The median for police supervisors and detectives was $69,310. However, the highest 10 percent for both categories earned much more: $72,450 and $104,410, respectively.

## Sites to Check Out

- **www.officer.com**—The site for everything law enforcement–related, including police-centered news articles, job postings, event schedules (basic sniper training anyone?), and an online store.

- **www.fbi.gov/wanted/topten/fugitives/fugitives.htm**—The FBI's Top Ten Most Wanted List.

- **www.sheriffs.org**—The National Sheriffs' Association Web site.

# Professional Football Player

**What You Do**

You will play football, running around with a small leather ball trying to make touchdowns in the opposing team's end zone. And when you do, a stadium full of fans will cheer and throw things. You'll also spend a lot of time training and practicing with your team.

**Why It's Risky**

Even though it's just a game, there is a lot on the line for professional players. There's the multimillion-dollar contract, sponsorships, and the ability to return to your home state to worry about. The guys on the other team are thinking the exact same thing, so every tackle is going to be bone-crushing—quite often literally. Spectator sports are rarely fatal, but you can count on a lot of painful injuries, like torn muscles and concussions. According to the U.S. Department of Labor, pro football players sustain nearly

Professional Football Player

eight times more injuries than any other commercial sports players.

### What You Need
The body and talent of a pro athlete. While you should always believe in the power of determination and hard work, this is one job that requires that extra spark you just have to be born with. You should have years of experience, including playing for a well-known college team.

### The Payoff
It's no secret that professional athletes make enormous sums of money. A football player's salary consists of an annual payout of their contract and a possible "signing bonus." The signing bonus is a one-time payment, but because of the NFL "hard" salary cap, the bonus is prorated over the life of the contract. The NFL salary cap is 59.5 percent of the total projected league revenue for the upcoming year, divided between the teams. For 2009, it will be about $123 million per team. Your percentage of that amount depends on how well you play and your popularity, but certainly we're talking seven figures. There are also plenty of awards you can win. For example, the Super Bowl MVP winner gets a new Cadillac of their choice.

However, player contracts are *not* guaranteed; they only apply if you remain on the team.

If you are cut, or leave, the balance of the contract is voided and you'll have to find another way to make millions of dollars.

### Sites to Check Out

- **www.nfl.com**—The National Football League Web site has everything any football fan or player needs to know, from tickets to highlight videos.

- **www.nflplayers.com**—The NFL Players Association Web site has news articles, videos, and player biographies.

- **www.espn.com**—ESPN is always on top of the latest sports news.

**Inspiration**

"Death is not the biggest fear we have; our biggest fear is taking the risk to be alive—the risk to be alive and express what we really are."

**—Don Miguel Ruiz**

# Pyrotechnician

### What You Do

First, you'll load up the fireworks from the plant and head to the site. There you'll meet your crew and begin preparing the launch area, a labor-intensive process that involves filling mortar boxes with sand and loading the shells into their tubes. When it's time for the show to start, you'll mostly be watching your laptop screen, which you should have coordinated with the devices to show what will be firing when. Then, after twenty minutes of flashing, booming glory, you'll pack everything up and call it a night.

### Why It's Risky

Around 10,000 Americans are treated in emergency rooms every Fourth of July for fireworks-related injuries. Granted, most of the missing hands and burned eyes are due to kids

Pyrotechnician

messing around with fireworks they have no idea how to use. But fireworks are explosives, and even professionals aren't invincible. If the mechanics malfunction, or a member of your crew loads a shell improperly, you could easily end up minus an arm, or worse. Even when everything is going smoothly, debris from the explosions will be falling directly on you and can cause burns or other injuries.

### The Payoff

You'll likely be paid on a show-by-show basis, receiving a percentage of the show's revenue. For a very small display, you may only make $100 profit, but for a major Independence Day celebration in a big city, expect to get $3,000 or more. Unless you work for an amusement park or some other facility with regular fireworks displays, gigs will be sporadic.

### What You Need

You should have knowledge of federal, state, and local laws pertaining to the proper handling of fireworks, and it's a good idea to work for a couple of years as a crew member to gain experience. Some states require you to be licensed, which may involve gathering letters of recommendation, taking a written exam, and obtaining a commercial driver's license with a hazardous materials endorsement to transport the explosives.

**Sites to Check Out**

- **www.pyroinnovations.com**—This company's site has helpful tips for becoming a pyrotechnician, and a fun Fireworks blog.

- **www.pyro-pages.com**—A site dedicated entirely to entertainment pyrotechnics.

- **www.fireworksnews.com**—To buy instruction manuals or DVDs, this is the site to visit.

## Ranch Hand

### What You Do

You'll take part in the day-to-day activities on the ranch, and your duties may change according to the season or day. This could include tractor mowing, tree trimming, keeping the ranch house and barn clean, loading hay, herding cattle, repairing fences, assisting calving, feeding animals, and carting stuff to and from the ranch.

### Why It's Risky

Your three main risks are machinery, animals, and weather. If you've ever seen a commercial tractor or thresher you can imagine how the blades could take off a finger or limb. The same goes for saw, grinders, and other tools you might use. As far as animals go, you wouldn't be the first hand to get thrown or kicked by a horse, or even head-butted by a goat. Think about this way: the people who do the Running

Ranch Hand

of the Bulls in Pamplona are around angry cows for one day—you'll be around them every day. There will be plenty of opportunities for you to get bruised or broken, possibly paralyzed. The weather can be your worst enemy, no matter where you work. It can be torture to lift heavy bags of seed in the summer on a ranch in Texas or Tennessee. Or you could be tending a sick heifer in sub-zero weather in Utah or Wyoming. Sure, there will be mild, beautiful days befitting a wildlife calendar, but you'll probably be shoveling manure.

### What You Need

You'll need some kind of agricultural experience, either from working on a ranch or farm or through an educational program. Numerous universities have a college of agriculture where you can prepare to manage a ranch yourself or learn more about the science behind ranching. You must be comfortable with horses and cattle, and know how to ride a horse. Ranch owners want someone who is dependable and punctual, plus sturdy enough to do hard labor year-round.

### The Payoff

The average ranch hand salary is $33,000/year. A lot of ranchers live in a house provided by the ranch owner, which may or may not be free. You should at least live nearby as work starts at sunrise and you don't want to have to commute at four in the morning.

### Sites to Check Out

- **www.ranchwork.com**—If you pay for a membership ($20–$40/month), you can post a résumé and look at job postings. It's basically Monster.com for cowboys.

- **www.ranchweather.com**—"We provide America's ranchers with the very best agricultural weather available!"

- **www.ffa.org**—The National FFA Organization, formerly known as Future Farmers of America, has grant and scholarship opportunities for those seeking an education in agriculture.

### Inspiration

"I must not fear. Fear is the mind-killer. Fear is the little-death that brings total obliteration. I will face my fear. I will permit it to pass over me and through me. And when it has gone past I will turn the inner eye to see its path. Where the fear has gone there will be nothing. Only I will remain."

—**Frank Herbert**

# Rodeo Clown

**What You Do**

It's your job to keep the bull rider from getting bludgeoned once he gets off (or falls off) the bull—and to do it in a way that makes this extremely perilous sport seem like fun and games. You'll have to dart back and forth, wave your arms, maybe jump in a barrel if the bull is coming at you and there's no other escape, all with two goals in mind: making the audience laugh and distracting the bull from creaming the dismounted rider. You'll also need to keep the audience entertained between rides with comedic skits or by bantering with the announcers.

**Why It's Risky**

Bulls often weigh up to 4,000 pounds and have horns designed to puncture flesh. And when they're mad, they're really, really mad. Scooter Culbertson is a rodeo clown who has broken twenty-four bones, suffered three concussions,

Rodeo Clown

dislocated his jaw, and lost an ear. If you're going to stand between two tons of angry bull and the rider who made him mad, chances are as throughout you're going to get hurt.

### What You Need
Agility, bravery (stupidity might work in a pinch), willingness to wear makeup and goofy pants, and a clown's sense of humor.

### The Payoff
$100 to $225 per show.

### Sites to Check Out
- **www.sankeyrodeo.com**—Learn about rodeo schools and purchase equipment.

- **www.twobulls.com**—This site includes a general store, information about TwoBulls Academy, and events sponsored by PBF, the Professional Bull Fighters organization.

## Roofer

### What You Do

You might be repairing roofs, replacing roofs, or laying brand-new roofs. These may involve helping the client decide on the best shingles and determining how many you'll need, possibly securing ladders or scaffolding, laying plywood over the rafters and covering it with a waterproof seal, and nailing or stapling the shingles in proper alignment to the roof.

### Why It's Risky

When you're climbing up and down steep roofs, it's very easy to slip and fall many feet to the ground. In addition, you'll be carrying heavy loads to and from, up and down the roof, and some of the materials you'll be using (tar, pitch, solvents) can be hazardous to your health. And finally, it's blazing hot on a roof in the middle of the summer; if you don't fall to your death, you might get some serious skin cancer if you don't slather on that sunscreen.

Roofer

### What You Need

It takes some agility to climb around on roofs, and it'll help if you know how to handle a nail gun. Hopefully you can avoid the mistake one Colorado worker made. He went to the dentist, complaining of a toothache and blurry vision. It turns out he had a four-inch nail embedded in his skull. Somehow he hadn't noticed when, a few days earlier, the nail gun backfired and sent a nail up through the roof of his mouth, narrowly missing his right eye.

### The Payoff

$14 to $20/hour.

### Sites to Check Out

- **www.roofing.com**—"The Community for Roofers and People with Roofs." More specifically, here you'll find classifieds, tips and techniques, resources, and discussions about the roofing business.

- **www.roofhelp.com**—A how-to site that includes a useful roofing glossary.

- **www.roofingfaq.com**—Questions? Ask the roofing expert!

## Security Guard

### What You Do

"Detect, deter, observe, and report" will become your mantra. You might work in a museum, shaking your finger at children climbing on the Rodin sculpture, or you might sit in the lobby of an office building, signing in messengers and watching the closed-circuit TV camera. What's so dangerous about that? Read on.

### Why It's Risky

It's your job to prevent crime, which means you're a prime target for criminals. It also means that if there's any sort of criminal activity, you'll probably have to get in the middle of it, at least until the cops arrive. While fatality rates in many industries are decreasing, death rates for security guards seem to be going up. If you don't get shot, stabbed, or otherwise attacked, you'll probably at least be working irregular hours, which wreaks havoc on sleep schedules.

Security Guard

### What You Need

Many security jobs only require that you be eighteen, undergo a background check, and go through basic training. If you're going to be armed, you'll need additional training and a license.

### The Payoff

Expect to make about $30,000/year.

### Sites to Check Out

- **www.securityguardservicesguide.com**— This site offers tips for folks looking to hire a security guard. It will give you useful insight into the hiring process and explain the many types of security positions and what they entail.

- **http://securityjobs.net**—Find job listings here.

- **http://isitrainingcenter.com**—Courses and seminars for prospective private security guards.

## Shark Cage Diver

### What You Do

You will dive into shark-infested waters protected by a rickety cage, possibly for research, photography, or an adrenaline high.

### Why It's Risky

It's only risky if you're the kind of person who thinks having all their limbs is "necessary." Sharks are beautiful creatures whose curiosity might urge them to find out what you taste like, and unfortunately, humans just aren't built to withstand their innocent nibbles. You will be chumming the waters to *attract* sharks, not just waiting to see if they show up. Feeding sharks rates pretty high on the dangerous scale.

### What You Need

Outfitting yourself for shark cage diving is very expensive. You'll need a boat, shark cage, crew, and scuba gear. The boat should be large enough

Shark Cage Diver

to drop and hoist the cage, plus have all of the equipment you'll need like a radio and navigation instruments. You'll also need a license for the boat and a slip at a local dock to keep it in. The crew should be experienced in the waters you're diving, whether it's your cameraperson or a fellow marine biologist. If you are not a skilled swimmer it would definitely be a good idea to pay for some lessons; swimming in deep, choppy water is much harder than doing laps in a pool. Yes, you'll be standing in a cage most of the time, but all it takes is a little trip to go overboard. The basic scuba certification course through PADI (Professional Association of Diving Instructors) is the most popular diving program worldwide and costs roughly $500.

### The Payoff

It's hard to calculate an across-the-board salary for shark cage divers. Start-up costs and fees are high, but vacationers pay a lot to endanger their lives. Your income also depends on the country you are sailing from, as an excursion from Cape Town costs customers about $200 USD, while one from Port Lincoln is $2,000. Big bonus? When you're not tempting the sharks, you could be enjoying the sun and sand of Mexico, Fiji, the Bahamas, South Africa, or Australia.

### Sites to Check Out

- **www.padi.com**—The PADI Web site has lots of great features like a dive shop locator, course descriptions, gear guides, and online classes.

- **www.flmnh.ufl.edu/fish/Sharks/ISAF/ISAF.htm**—The International Shark Attack File keeps track of all known attacks from the mid-1500s to the present. You can print out their Shark Attack Questionnaire and just keep it with you.

- **www.sharkcagediving.net**—Web site for South African Great White shark diving tour with the "legendary Brian McFarlane." Boasts only one trip without a shark in the past three years.

**Inspiration**

"Nothing in life is to be feared. It is only to be understood."

**—Marie Curie**

**Sherpa**

### What You Do

You'll be a guide for eager tourists and adventurers, leading them on extreme hikes and camping trips. Traditionally, sherpas are locals of the Himalayan region who take folks up Mt. Everest and the surrounding mountains. However, the term "sherpa" is used increasingly for guides in any part of the world who are familiar with the terrain they lead hikers through. You'll help carry equipment, set up camp at night, and provide aid for injured hikers as needed.

### Why It's Risky

Hikers don't usually require guides unless the terrain is particularly treacherous. Cliffs, hungry wild animals, falling rocks, high elevations, unpredictable weather, and avalanches are just a few of the threats you're likely to face.

Sherpa

### What You Need

You'll need to know the area you're covering better than the palm of your hand. If you could get lost, you've failed as a sherpa. You'll also need to be very fit, adept at outdoorsman skills, and if you're good at shaping group dynamics, you'll make the adventure pleasanter for all involved (folks who are hungry, tired, wet, sore, and cold tend to make for bad company).

### The Payoff

If you're an honest to goodness sherpa in the Himalayas, you're probably only making $7 to $10 a day (granted, that's worth a bit more in Tibet, but still . . .). However, sherpas in the United States make anywhere from $10 to over $100 an hour, depending on the difficulty of the outing, how many people you're guiding, and whether you're working for another adventure company or starting your own mountaineering guide business.

### Sites to Check Out

- **www.backdoorjobs.com/adventure.html**—You'll find all sorts of adventure guide jobs here.

- **www.coolworks.com**—This site also has a lot of mountaineering job listings.

- **www.abc-of-mountaineering.com**—Here is a wealth of information about all things mountaineering.

## Smoke Jumper

### What You Do

Parachute from an airplane into a forest fire, where other firefighters can't reach you. Food and water will follow once you've landed, so you're self-sufficient for two full days of fighting the fire. In about three to five days, once the fire's more under control, you and your fellow smoke jumpers will pack up your stuff (approximately 100 pounds of it) and hoof it back to the nearest road, which could be a long and not-so-leisurely stroll.

### Why It's Risky

You're plummeting from an airplane into the vicinity of a raging inferno. Is there anything *not* risky about that? Not to be a pessimist, but there is the chance that your parachute might not open, or you could light up like a human candle. You could inhale a lot of smoke. The plane could explode. You could land in a

Smoke Jumper

flaming skeleton of a Douglas fir! You are in a very seriously deadly situation, with only your wits and a few buddies to watch your back. If the regular risks of firefighting are not enough to keep your adrenaline pumping, this might be your solution.

### What You Need
You'll need a good deal of firefighting experience: at least one season of fighting wildfires, on top of at least one year of related work (as a park ranger or farmer, for example) or a minimum of twenty-four semester hours studying relevant academic subjects (like forestry or range/wildlife management). You've got to be between 5'0" and 6'5" and 120–200 pounds, have sharp vision and hearing, and work your booty through boot camp. And then, prepare yourself for five weeks of very rigorous parachuting training. If you pass the physical requirements, you're not quite off the hook; you need to be mentally and emotionally stable, able to think independently and on your feet, and be constantly aware of your surroundings.

### The Payoff
$16–$24/hour, plus 25 percent hazard pay on extra dangerous, uncontrolled wildfire missions.

**Sites to Check Out**

- **www.fs.fed.us/fire/people/smokejumpers**—
  All you'll need to know about becoming a
  smoke jumper.

- **www.jobmonkey.com/parks/html/smoke-
  jumpers.html**—Smoke-jumping jobs.

- **http://alaskasmokejumpers.com/index.
  html**—Straight talk from one of the nation's
  few smoke-jumping bases.

## Stunt Double

### What You Do

You get to do all the things that are too dangerous (or difficult) for actors or actresses to do, like get hit by cars, jump through windows, or hop onto a moving train. Often, actors are contractually prohibited from performing stunts that will threaten their physical well-being. Other times, the actors are simply not capable of doing something the scene demands. So a stunt double of similar appearance is hired to do the job.

### Why It's Risky

If it weren't risky, probably the actor would do it him- or herself. Of course, some stunts are more dangerous than others. You might find yourself simply kneeling on a hard floor for an hour, because the actress didn't want to bruise her knees during the confession scene, or you might end up spread-eagled on the hood of a burning Chevy, hoping the cameraman gets his shots in a hurry.

Stunt Double

## What You Need

The more agile, strong, and willing to put yourself in harm's way you are, the more likely you'll be to land a well-paying gig. And if you have special skills (acrobatic or martial arts training, snowboarding experience, you're really good at falling on your head, etc.), you'll have an edge on your competition. You'll also get more jobs, and more money for those jobs, once you become a Screen Actors Guild (SAG) member. On a more mundane note, you'll also need head shots and a résumé to mail to the stunt coordinator of any production you're interested in being a part of.

## The Payoff

This will vary, depending on how dangerous your stunt is, but you'll probably get what's called "hazard pay," which is around $500/day for a moderately dangerous gig. Don't expect to work every day, though. Gigs for stunt doubles are likely to be inconsistent: It's not unusual to have two solid weeks of work and then a month of nothing.

## Sites to Check Out

- **www.stuntperformer.co.nz**—This New Zealand stunt performer's personal site has a lot of helpful information. Check out the FAQ page.

# Tornado Chaser

**What You Do**

You'll travel around, trying your darndest to get caught in the middle of a life-threatening storm system. Your expeditions could be for research purposes, scientific field programs, storm photography, self-education, commercial video opportunities, or new media coverage. Or because it's a cool thing to tell people at a party: "What do you do?" "I'm an accountant. You?" "I chase tornados." Try it.

**Why It's Risky**

Well, heavy winds, for starters. And with that comes hail, rain, flooding, lightning, etc. There's a reason most people evacuate when tornadoes come through, rather than race toward them.

**What You Need**

A good truck (or bus, if you're doing a tour) that won't break down in the middle of a chase, and plenty of knowledge on meteorology and

Tornado Chaser

forecasting. Depending on your goals, you may also want a laptop, walkie-talkies, cell phones, a GPS system, camera, or video camera.

### The Payoff

Compensation will vary significantly, depending on what you do with your chasing experiences (selling artwork vs. scientific data, for example). Another possibility is to start your own tornado tour business, to share the adrenaline rush with all the other crazy folks out there who want to know what it's like to be really close to a twister. Charge between $1,000 to $3,000 per tour, which could last up to a week (that price would include lodging for your clients, but if you have twenty people on your tour, you can still make a hefty profit). Keep in mind that you'll need good insurance for your business, and tornado season is only April through July.

### Sites to Check Out

- **www.chasingstorms.com**—The National Association of Storm Chasers and Spotters offers safety alerts, photos, and lots of information.

- **www.nssl.noaa.gov**—The National Severe Storms Laboratory, headquartered in Norman, Oklahoma, offers field observations and tips for careers in related areas.

- **www.stormchase.us**—Resources for weather enthusiasts and storm chasers.

# Tower Technician

**What You Do**

You are the hero who keeps society connected. You climb hundreds of feet to the tops of towers to maintain and repair the equipment that makes texting and television possible. You will often be away from home for weeks at a time.

**Why It's Risky**

Cell phone towers can be up to 500 feet tall, and radio and TV towers can get up to 1,500 feet. While you're provided with safety equipment, such as harnesses and safety clips, there's often pressure to get the job done quickly, which means that safety is frequently compromised. There will be very little room to stand once you're up there, and since you'll be working with electrical equipment, there's always the risk of shock. Weather can get nasty quickly, too, and everyone knows that tall metal structures are lightning magnets.

Tower Technician

### What You Need

You'll need to be strong enough to haul yourself up a massive tower with over twenty pounds of equipment in tow. Even if you're elevated via a power lift, you'll need some muscle to move around the tools, machinery, and parts. Electrical experience is a plus. While you don't need a license to be a tower tech, you will need extensive safety training, especially if you do not want to die.

### The Payoff

$16–$27/hour.

### Sites to Check Out

- **www.tbo.com/news/nationworld/MGB-SQA8IS6F.html**—"The Most Lethal Job in America," an article about life (and death) as a tower tech.

- **www.simplyhired.com/job-id/gjkxcu5hpt/tower-technician-jobs**—Tower technician job listings.

- **www.steelintheair.com/Blog/celltowerinfoblog.html**—Useful cell tower information and relevant news

## Truck Driver

### What You Do

As a truck driver (or "trucker," "teamster," or, if you're in Canada, "truckie") you'll drive long hours, transporting goods or materials from manufacturing plants to stores or distribution centers. You'll probably also be responsible for the inspection and maintenance of your truck.

### Why It's Risky

When you're driving long hours on boring highways, it's easy to fall asleep at the wheel. And though sleeping at a truck stop is safer than sleeping while you're driving, many a teamster has had a rude awakening when his truck was pillaged in the wee hours of the morning. Icy roads add to driving risks, of course, and there's always the possibility that your brakes will give out on a long windy downhill . . . Oh, and be careful changing tires or uncoupling the trailer from the cab. You wouldn't be the first driver to get crushed under forty tons of metal, rubber, and cargo.

### What You Need

If you want to drive the big rigs (eighteen-wheelers), you'll have to be at least eighteen to drive locally, or twenty-one to drive cross-country. You'll also need to take and pass an exam to get your CDL (Commercial Driver's License).

### The Payoff

You might make anywhere from \$.19 to \$.44/mile, after training. Since there's a strict legal limit to the number of hours you can drive, expect to make \$35,000–\$40,000 in your first year. And you'll get to travel a lot!

Truck Driver

**Sites to Check Out**

- **www.thetruckersreport.com**—Everything truck-related, including trucker poems.

- **www.truckdriver.com**—You can fill out one application to apply to multiple companies on this site.

- **www.dmv.org**—At "The Unofficial Guide to the DMV" you can find links to CDL licensing information, commercial driving education, and commercial driver FAQs in your state.

## Lingo

*Alligator*—A blown-out tire casing.

*Chicken Coop*—A weigh station (which usually has a very small office).

*Double Nickel*—Fifty-five miles per hour.

*Flip-Flop*—U-turn or return trip.

*Owner-operators* (O/Os) own the trucks they drive and are often self-employed independent contractors (as opposed to company drivers, who work for a company that provides the truck).

*Pickle Park*—A rest area (your guess is as good as mine).

*Smokey Bear (or just "bear")*—Either the fuzzy Forest Service mascot or, more likely, a police officer (Smokey's broad-brimmed cap bears a strong resemblance to a cop's campaign hat).

# United Nations Peacekeeper

**What You Do**

United Nations peacekeepers, also known as "blue helmets," compose the Department of Peacekeeping Operations. This department, formed in 1948, is composed usually of soldiers, police officers, doctors, nurses, pilots, engineers, administrators, economists, legal experts, de-miners, electoral observers, human rights monitors, specialists in civil affairs and governance, humanitarian workers, and experts in communications and public information. So there's a lot of diversity in the field. You could be sewing up a wounded soldier or flying a helicopter full of food for refugees.

**What You Need**

Aspiring peacekeepers must be U.S. citizens with five years of experience in professional law enforcement. You'll also have to pass a physical agility test that includes: the "low

UN Peacekeeper

hurdle," the "12-foot tunnel run," the "dummy drag," and the "ladder climb with shotgun."

## Why It's Risky

UN peacekeepers are sent into high-risk areas of armed conflict with the main objective of restoring and maintaining peace. Nevertheless, over the years, the UN peacekeeper mission has evolved and no longer consists of only maintaining cease-fires, but rather has a much more multidimensional mission. Focus has shifted to the implementation of peace agreements in areas of conflict. Some positions are more dangerous than others, but since the creation of the DPKO Union in 1948, there have been a total of 2,545 registered fatalities.

## The Payoff

Each member country pays their peacekeepers according to their national rank and salary scales. The UN then reimburses the country a little over $1,000/month per peacekeeper.

## Sites to Check Out

- **www.un.org/Depts/dpko/dpko/**—The United Nation Peacekeeping official Web site.

- **www.slate.com/id/2146479/**—An interesting article on how to become a UN peacekeeper.

# Underwater Welder

### What You Do

Dive twenty-five to 100 feet underwater to install or repair pipes, underwater structures (like the bases of bridges or tunnels), boat bottoms, or even a nuclear power plant. You'll be following the blueprint instructions to cut metal (using oxyfuel, an abrasive water jet, or mechanical cutting equipment), fit it, inspect it (possibly using ultrasonic and radiological technology), and maybe even take pictures of it (underwater photography and videography).

### Why It's Risky

First, it's really hard to see underwater. With strong currents, debris, and very little light, your welding buddy could almost as easily saw apart your wrist as the pipeline. Currents will also threaten to sweep you away, so be sure to tie yourself to a boat or well-planted object before diving in. And when you're using electrical

Underwater Welder

equipment in the water, shock is always a possibility.

**What You Need**

You'll need commercial diving skills and a welder license. If you don't have prior commercial diving experience, consider going to a commercial diving school, where you'll become familiar with diving equipment, underwater physiology, safety, rigging, and communication. You'll also need a physical; spending lots of time deep beneath the water's surface takes a toll on the body, and you have to be in good shape to make it.

**The Payoff**

Welder/divers are generally paid by the job rather than by the hour or year, but if you can get regular work of medium difficulty, expect to make from $60,000 to $100,000/year.

**Sites to Check Out**

- **www.aws.org/education/plunge.html**—The American Welding Society discusses underwater welding.

- **www.underwater.com**—This online magazine has a wide range of articles about diving, including a very informative piece on underwater welders.

- **www.commercialdivingacademy.com**—A commercial diving school offering courses in underwater welding.

## Weight Lifter

### What You Do

Weight lifting dates back to ancient Egypt and Greece, where early weight lifting took the forms of lifting heavy stones, statues, or even bags of sand. It's not that different today, though most weight lifters use barbells (which weigh between 15 to 20 kg. or 35 to 45 lbs.), and adding weight discs between 56 to 105 kg. (124 to 231 lbs.) for men and 48 to 70 kg. (105 to 154 lbs) for women.

### Why It's Risky

Like the Hungarian weightlifter Janos Baranyai during his first Olympics, you just might end up dislocating an elbow, or worse. Studies have linked aneurysms, torn aortas, and glaucoma to weight lifting. And if you should drop one of those honking weights on your toe, stomach, or face, you'll sustain serious damage.

Weight Lifter

### What You Need

You'll need determination and a whole lot of strength, which comes from hours of training. In addition, you'll want to join the USA Weightlifting Association and/or a local club affiliated with USA Weightlifting. You'll also need to find a coach who is certified through USA Weightlifting.

### The Payoff

In 2001 weight lifter Sergo Chakhoyan got a $25,000 bonus for breaking a world record for weight lifting in the Goodwill Games. He also won a few medals, and $2,000 for each of them. He walked away with $31,000—not bad for a day's work. Of course, how much you earn will depend on how much you win. If you're looking for a steadier income, you might consider coaching, which, depending on your qualifications and experience, could earn you anywhere from $25,000 to $150,000.

### Sites to Check Out

- **www.weightlifting.teamusa.org**—The USA Weightlifting Association.

- **www.iwf.net**—The International Weightlifting Federation.

- **www.cscca.org**—The Collegiate Strength and Conditioning Coaches Association.

## Window Washer

### What You Do

You'll work in an urban area, hanging from the sides of skyscrapers so that people can look out of crystal-clear windows. There are also residential washers, who mainly use ladders. You, or someone from your company, will evaluate the job for safety concerns and pricing.

### Why It's Risky

The obvious concern when washing windows is that you could fall to your death. On December 7, 2007, the Moreno brothers were washing an apartment building in uptown Manhattan when they fell forty-seven floors. One brother, miraculously, survived. They tried to ride their platform to the ground after the scaffolding collapsed, but Edgar Moreno was thrown off and died. However, neither were wearing their safety harnesses. Alcides Moreno had fifteen different operations and his hospital bills were

Window Washer

in the millions, but he can now speak and will probably walk again. His survival is a medical mystery.

Some nonfatal risks include exposure to dangerous chemicals, smog, and bad weather.

### What You Need
You can start out as an apprentice or assistant to a senior washer. As such, you'll learn the different chemicals, equipment, and safety precautions. There will be a lot of lifting and washing, so you'll need a strong back and arm muscles.

### The Payoff
Your salary depends on what kind of work you do and your experience. Commercial work is year-round and pays reasonably well, while residential work is seasonal and more lucrative. A seasoned washer can work more efficiently, thus making more money. One washer was paid $1,500 for an office park job that he finished in only three days. He not only made $500 a day but was also able to take on other jobs later in the week.

### Sites to Check Out
- **www.iwca.org**—"The International Window Cleaning Association is a non-profit trade 501(c)(6) association committed to raising

the standards of professionalism within the window cleaning industry."

- **www.windowacademy.com**—A Web site run by two experienced washers, Chris and Bobby, provides training packages, window-washing tips, and a forum.

## Inspiration

"Only when we are no longer afraid do we begin to live."

**—Dorothy Thompson**

"Don't be afraid to go out on a limb. That's where the fruit is."

**—H. Jackson Browne**

## Resources

Here are some additional Web sites to aid you in your dangerous job search:

- **www.backdoorjobs.com**—Exciting jobs, internships, and volunteer positions around the world.

- **www.lookingforadventure.com**—Find links to adventurous career opportunities.

- **www.great-adventures.com**—Search for jobs by country.

- **www.oapn.net**—The Outdoor Adventure Professional Network.

- **http://wilderdom.com/jobs**—Has job listings in outdoor, environmental, and adventure education.

- **http://thetravelersnotebook.com**—Articles and ideas about travel and adventure jobs.

- **www.coolworks.com**—Find exciting seasonal work here.

If you're looking to start your own business, check out these links to get started:

- **www.entrepreneur.com** is a wellspring of helpful articles and information for starting and running a business.

- **www.eventuring.org** is the Kauffman Foundation's guide to building innovative companies, with stories, how-to's, and a glossary of terms.

- **www.tannedfeet.com** is almost overwhelming it has so much information for entrepreneurs of all sorts.

- **www.benlore.com**—The Entrepreneur's Mind offers in-depth profiles of successful entrepreneurs and tells the stories of how they got to where they are.

- **http://sethgodin.typepad.com** is the blog of highly successful entrepreneurial guru Seth Godin. Read it for wisdom and inspiration.

- **www.sba.gov/hotlist/license.html** has links to business license information, listed by state.

- **www.irs.org** is the site to visit for a tax identification number.

- **www.business.gov**—You'll want to check this site out for federal and state licenses, tax information, and other resources listed by subject.

- **www.governmentguide.com**—Here you can type your zip code into the My Personalized Guide box and then click on Small Business to find the regulations for your city or town (although searches for smaller towns may not yield any results).

# Acknowledgments

The more I learn about writing and publishing, the more I realize that creating a book is really a team effort. For this book I am indebted to a very creative, talented, and hard-working crew.

Huge thanks to Tony Lyons for the idea for *Dangerous Jobs*, as well as for all the opportunities and support he offers. To the rest of the Skyhorse team, including Bill Wolfsthal, Adam Bozarth, and Kathleen Go, thank you for using your diverse skills to help design, correct, and sell this project of mine. I'm so glad to be working with you all. Colette Becker, Janike Ruginis, Louisa Stratigis, and John Kang—your names should really be on the cover of this book along with mine. Many, many thanks for your assistance with research and writing.

To all the folks who shared stories of their dangerous job experiences with me, thank you and good luck staying alive. You're nuts to do what you do. But then again, most of us are for one reason or another.

Thanks to my family for instilling in me a sense of adventure, as well as the responsibility and courage to discover and do what we're meant to with our lives.

Finally, thanks to my husband Tim, who encourages me in my all my various and sundry pursuits. I pray I never take for granted all that you give me.

# About the Author

Abigail R. Gehring is currently a writer and managing editor and has previously been about twenty-three other things, including a dancer, a "Cinderella," a snowboard instructor, and a lipstick reader. She considers the fact that she's held one job for every year of her young life (and many for only a day or less) to be a sign of her versatility and adventurous spirit, rather than an indication of incompetency or commitment issues (if you have any doubt, ask her mother). She is the author of *Odd Jobs: 101 Ways to Make an Extra Buck* and the editor of *Back to Basics: A Complete Guide to Traditional Skills, Third Edition*. She lives in Edgewater, New Jersey, but grew up in Wilmington, Vermont and still prefers to consider herself a Vermonter.